"I absolutely love this book! It is definitely chicken soup for your soul. I couldn't stop turning the pages. It is part memoir, part adventure story, and part personal and spiritual development guide. Do yourself a really big favor and read this book."
—Jack Canfield, coauthor of the #1 *New York Times* best-selling *Chicken Soup for the Soul®* series

"Kim Sorrelle's meditation on what it means to truly live out biblical love frequently takes her to one of the most challenging countries on earth in which to apply it, her mission field of Haiti. Those concerned about that country's ongoing humanitarian crisis will find here vivid stories of people putting love to work on the grittiest ground, suffused with gentle humor, steely resolve, and the author's undeniable courage."
—Charles Honey, editor-in-chief and writer at School News Network and religion editor and columnist, *The Grand Rapids Press*/MLive

"Life-changing for the author translated to life-changing for me. So insightful, powerful, and funny. The perfect blend of inspiration and entertainment. I couldn't put it down."
—Dennis Bell, former NBA player with the New Yor~~k~~ ~~cks~~

"*Love Is* removes the blinders from y ~~...~~
new sense of compassion and possibi~~...~~
refreshingly honest and inspiring boo~~...~~
—Steve Harrison, Publis~~...~~ *Interview Report*

"Leaning on humor and heartache and grace, Kim Sorrelle illuminates Scripture in ways that help us to know love in vibrant new ways—most significantly as a living, breathing being. She reminds us of the power in being unconditionally open, vulnerable, and human. Read it with a highlighter in one hand and tissue in the other."
—Tom Rademacher, longtime columnist for *The Grand Rapids Press*

"This life-changing, life-challenging book is both funny and inspirational. It's a good read for anyone in business. Having great relationships with staff, coworkers, customers, and vendors takes the kind of love that Kim writes about."

—Dr. Ivan Misner, Founder of Business Network International and
New York Times best-selling author

"We've all heard the 'Love Chapter' in 1 Corinthians 13 many times, but never like this. I can't remember the last time I was so sucked in to storytelling in a nonfiction book. Kim Sorrelle invites her readers around the campfires of Haiti (where she would sleep in abject fear under a crude picnic table), to a crocodile-filled lake in Hispaniola, and the presidential palace of Venezuela. In her openhearted, relatable, and often hilarious way, Kim winsomely teaches us to 'live love' in a whole new way, with a whole new mindset."

—Lorilee Craker, author of fifteen books, including the *New York Times* best seller *Through the Storm* with Lynne Spears, *Money Secrets of the Amish*, and *Anne of Green Gables, My Daughter and Me*

"In a tightly composed structure, Kim Sorrelle presents the reader with fourteen attributes of love based on St. Paul's famous description in 1 Corinthians, chapter 13. Sorrelle's anecdotes are amazing revelations of her character, and the reader cannot help but admire her pluck and courage, as well as her dedication to work in Haiti."

—The Rev. Dr. Karin Orr, Chaplain,
Clark Retirement Community

"Kim Sorrelle has written a charming and challenging, engaging and energizing book that takes us back to the most basic element of being human: love. Her journey becomes all of our journeys, as she teaches us what living out love looks like every minute of every day. Thank you, Kim!"

—Ann Byle, freelance writer for *Publisher's Weekly*

LOVE IS

LOVE IS

A Yearlong Experiment of Living Out

1 Corinthians 13 Love

Kim Sorrelle

KREGEL
PUBLICATIONS

Published by Kregel Publications, a division of Kregel Inc., 2450 Oak Industrial Dr. NE, Grand Rapids, MI 49505.

Cataloging-in-Publication Data is available from the Library of Congress.

ISBN 978-0-8254-4674-0, print
ISBN 978-0-8254-7724-9, epub

Printed in the United States of America
21 22 23 24 25 26 27 28 29 30 / 5 4 3 2 1

To the one who has taught me the most about whom to love, when to love, and how to love, because she loves everyone always, unconditionally—my daughter, Amanda.

Contents

WHY LOVE?

A COUPLE OF YEARS AGO, I read an article about a man who committed to living a year like Jesus. Wow. How transformational! To have that peace and joy—or is it tough and gritty? Either way, all ways, life would never be the same.

I thought about how I would brave that task. How would I know that I was really living like Jesus?

Then the light bulb blazed: God *is* love. So to live like Jesus would be living love. But what is love? And how would I live that while crossing cultural obstacles with one foot on US soil and the other in places like Haiti, where love is both abundant and seemingly nonexistent, challenging and effortless simultaneously?

I know some things about love. It is universal, timeless, and ageless. It is a feeling, a choice, a given. It is all-encompassing, enduring, and everlasting. Love conquers all, never fails, and keeps us together. But it hurts, gets lost, and takes time.

There are love bugs, love seats, and love boats. There are love notes, love songs, and lovebirds.

Love is a dare, a game, a language. You can be lovesick, loveless, and lovely.

You can fall in love, be addicted to love, do anything in the name of love, play the game of love, use the power of love.

You can't hurry it or buy it and you don't know if it will be there tomorrow. Yet love is all you need.

There's even a Love Chapter of the Bible.

We've heard the Love Chapter (1 Cor. 13:4–8) read and expounded upon many times (mostly at weddings). It's one of the most memorized, admired, and well-known passages in all of Scripture, even by non-church folk. In fact, we've heard this famous passage so often our eyes kind of glaze over. "Love is patient, love is kind, does not env . . ." *Yeah, yeah. We know how this goes.*

But what is love, really?

John says that God is love. Bob the Tomato of VeggieTales® says God is bigger than the boogie man, Godzilla, and the monsters on TV. So the love that is God must be way bigger than my love of black licorice and movie theater popcorn.

Jesus named the number one law, of all of the laws—and there were tons. Leviticus, the third book of the Torah and the Old Testament, lists most of the 613 rules of conduct God gave to Israel. Jesus could have picked any one of them. Murder is pretty heavy. Stealing isn't exactly harmless. Adultery can destroy families in a hurry. Lying about someone could get you and them into a heap of trouble. But with no hesitation, he picked the one that sat right in between "don't carry a grudge or seek revenge" and "don't mate two different kinds of animals." Jesus basically said, "That's an easy one. Love God and love people" (see Lev. 19:18). Just like that. There is no exception clause, no fine print, no room for interpretation. Love people, all of them, every single one.

Even deeper, Paul said that you can't go wrong if you love people because love is the fulfilling of the law. An order gets picked out of the warehouse, loaded, delivered, fulfilled. "Fulfilled" is complete, buttoned-up, stick a fork in it, done. All of it, all 613 laws, if you love (as in, the love that God is), you don't break laws. So WWJD (what would Jesus do) is interchangeable with WWLD (what would love do).

If you understand love and live love, your life will change. If that love gets a little contagious, the whole world could be a better place.

I am going to figure out love one word at a time, taking 1 Corinthians 13 to heart and feet. Live it, learn it, love it. It is quite a list, a list that I think I already know, but somehow I think I have a lot to learn.

> Love is patient, love is kind. It does not envy, it does not boast, it is not proud. It does not dishonor others, it is not self-seeking, it is not easily angered, it keeps no record of wrongs. Love does not delight in evil but rejoices with the truth. It always protects, always trusts, always hopes, always perseveres.
>
> Love never fails. (1 Cor. 13:4–8)

CHAPTER 1

LOVE IS PATIENT

LOVE IS EVERYWHERE, FROM SITCOMS to reality shows, T-shirts to best sellers. Heart-shaped this and kiss, kiss that. Raymond gets it from everybody, Patty wants to find it for her millionaires, and the new Bachelor is trying to uncover it somewhere in a hot tub full of bikinis.

Love: "little word, little white bird," says Carl Sandburg. Love, "little word, little pain in the neck," says me. I thought living love as outlined in 1 Corinthians 13 would be simple: just walk in love, speak in love, and act in love. But for such a small word, love is hard to do. It's also multilayered. Take patience, for example, love's first requirement.

In the last couple of days, I have yelled at a space-hogging car and shown my frustration with the Chatty Cathy cashier at the grocery store. *All I wanted to do was go home and eat, dagnabit!* I was short when a staff meeting veered from my personal agenda. Then the word hit me, and love slapped me across the face: Patience—love's first definition in the passage.

Patience: 1. the quality of being patient, as the bearing of provocation, annoyance, misfortune, or pain, without complaint, loss of temper, irritation, or the like. 2. an ability or willingness to suppress restlessness or annoyance when confronted with delay: to have patience with a slow learner. 3. quiet, steady perseverance; even-tempered care; diligence: to work with patience.

Is impatience genetic? If it is, I am in trouble. One time, my spitfire, type A, go-to-work-with-the-flu father told me that he "prided himself on his patience." Huh? Really? I loved my dad to pieces, and he had many excellent qualities, but patience was not one of them. He taught me if you want a job done right, just do it yourself; poky people should not be allowed in the fast lane; and eleven items at the ten-items-and-under checkout is unacceptable.

Hurry! Get it done. Do it faster. Slow is useless. Pull yourself up by your bootstraps. No whining, you're fine.

So, between my possible genetic predisposition and my somewhat harried, hurried personality, it would not come naturally if patience came. God is patient. I am not. But I can't just skip over love's first definition, can I? My goal for this month is to walk, speak, act, and be patient. I will even pray for patience, which scares me to death because God will likely answer that prayer. *How* he will answer it scares me. Still, here goes:

Oh, Lord, help me acquire patience. Help me to learn and act in patient love. And please be gentle.

Welcome to Haiti

Flying over Haiti is like flying over Jurassic Park. You see the lush mountains slowly rolling out into gorgeous, green plains and finally the sandy fringe of the turquoise Caribbean, but you don't see the carnivorous monsters waiting to devour whoever dares to land.

On my first visit to Haiti in 2000, I vowed never to return. The thick poverty was so suffocating that it made the fumes from an oil-guzzling diesel truck seem like pure oxygen. But Haiti had my number and my heart. People say it's an addictive country to visit: once in Haiti, there's something about the Haitians, the history, and even the air that can get in your blood and draw you back time and again. Within six months of returning home, I was tasting the perpetually dusty air again. Today, the poverty is thicker, the oxygen is thinner, and so are the people.

After seeing so much need in Haiti, my spitfire dad and I started a nonprofit organization called Rays of Hope International. First under the umbrella of the organization that I was directing, Careforce International, then independently when a diagnosis required my resignation.

Pancreatic cancer gifted my husband an early ticket to heaven in March of 2009. Breast cancer gifted me a new bustline the very same year. By late December, having finished all surgeries, treatments, and *Grey's Anatomy* episodes, it was time to get off the couch and get back to work.

As fate would have it, Rays of Hope needed a bookkeeper, making for an easy transition from potato to productive. But what began as part-time bean counting morphed into a twelve-hours-a-day, seven-days-a-week marathon when an earthquake shook Haiti like a paint mixer. Within a couple of weeks, my Keds landed on what used to be solid ground in Port au Prince.

Even losing my husband did not diminish my passion for Haiti and Haitians. Somehow, taking a cannonball to the heart galvanized the steely part of me that wanted purpose in my life. Widowhood at forty-seven brought me to my knees, but love for the wrecked little nation lifted me back up in the bluest of waters. But even on my first visit, when I fought falling in love with Haiti, I knew my love would require patience such as I had never needed before.

Patient love. Love is patient. Long-suffering. Unwearied. Unflappable. But what if a situation makes you prickle with irritation like a hedgehog? Or what if the spiky circumstances don't change for a really long time, longer than you think you can handle? And how can someone practice patience in a country where horns are continually honking, dogs are forever barking, and a five-mile drive can take an hour?

My beloved Haiti has stretched my patience over and over, but maybe never so much as during January's Mixed-Up Shipping Container Incident.

Rays of Hope fills and ships 40-foot containers full of resources into a country in drastic need. Medical supplies take up the majority of the 2,250 cubic feet of space. School supplies, dental tools, and mattresses for orphanages usually take up the rest. Everything we ship goes to organizations that are working to show compassion and love to others. The container gets loaded on a 40-foot-long chassis that is then pulled by a semitruck to Detroit. There the container rides on the rails to New Jersey, where a crane takes it off the flatcar and loads it onto a massive ship with lots and lots of other containers full of lots and lots of stuff. The ship sets sail and eventually pulls into the port in Port au Prince, where another crane picks it up and sets it down on Haitian ground.

Shipping is the easy part. Getting the container released by the Haitian government? Now that requires unflappability the likes of which most humans are not naturally blessed. Over and over, my patience has been tested, fried, and fricasseed in the fires of Haitian Red Tape (capitalization required, trust me). But this incident was award-winning ("and the Oscar for Patience goes to . . .").

The plan was that Patrick, our Haitian manager, would pick me up at 9:30 a.m. We would then make our way to the port, get the container, and have it hauled to our warehouse, where we should arrive about 11 a.m. We planned to finish unloading the cargo by 3 p.m. and then head up to Borel, arriving shortly before sunset at 6 p.m., meet up with friends and work partners, and crash for the night, so we could start a project there bright and early the next morning.

The reality was different from those best-laid plans. I woke up in the wee, dark hours to the tormented sounds of Jude, one of the young boys at Notre Maison Orphanage, my home away from home in Port au Prince. "Aaaaa!" he cried out. Notre Maison is a home for children with disabilities, and it also has a few beds for visitors.

"Aaaaaa . . ." Three seconds long, plus a one-second pause.

"Aaaaa . . ."

Poor little guy. I felt for him, but I decided there was no sleeping through Jude's sounds in the dark.

I gave up and prepared my breakfast of coffee, watermelon, and supremely tart oranges. Miraculously, the power was on, so I grabbed my laptop to return emails for the next couple of hours.

By 9:17, I had freshened up, applied a little makeup, stuck some bobby pins in my hair, and filled my backpack. Ten minutes later, the power went "poof," to no one's surprise, so I joined my friend Shirley on the roof of the orphanage to wait for Patrick.

Shirley had already been in Haiti for ten days and planned to stay and serve for three months. We swapped stories and talked about faith, love, and our beloved Haiti. We talked about the power—would it come back on within the next hour, day, or week?

Patrick arrived a little after 11 a.m.

"Good mornin'!" He was all smiles. "The container is all set. The broker is getting it right now so we can go straight to the warehouse."

"Great!" I was thrilled. "Let's go."

I turned to help Shirley figure out an app on her iPhone, and when I swiveled around again, Patrick was gone.

"Patrick!" I bellowed his name to the surrounding area, my heart sinking just a little. Something in me knew he was not waiting in the car or using the bathroom.

"He left to go get minutes," I heard from a disembodied voice on street level. My heart dropped a few more inches.

Minutes, as in mobile phone minutes, resemble lottery scratch-off tickets, and, like phone chargers, cold drinks, and plantain chips, are available on most street corners. You trade the street vendor 100 gourdes for a card he retrieves from his red apron, scratch off the entry code with a coin, and punch the code into your cell phone. Voila! You can make calls.

I had no idea why Patrick left to get minutes at that time. In the twenty miles between Notre Maison and the warehouse, there would be a sea of red aprons full of scratch-off cards and mobile minutes. I sighed, but on the scale of one to ten, with rasping, guttural sighing being a ten and the slightest exhale being a one, I was only at about a four. However, the day was young. Haiti had taught me to be reasonably plucky in the face of irritating circumstances, at least those that occur before noon. But we were already hours behind schedule.

Patrick returned just before noon, and we jumped in the car to head out for the day. (Haiti time: 9:30 a.m., 11:51 a.m. = What's the difference?) *Love is patient. Patience is love.*

"Hey Patrick, did you call everyone on the distribution list to meet us at the warehouse?"

"Yeah, Kim, I did all that already."

I had an instinct. "OK, so did you get ahold of everyone?"

"Well, not everyone."

I skimmed the distribution list to see the names of those anxiously waiting for the goods that left our dock in Grand Rapids, Michigan, in April, nine months beforehand. They would be happy that customs finally released the container.

It didn't always take this long.

It usually didn't take this long.

It was painful that it had taken this long, but now—praise God—the container was on its way to the warehouse, cleared by customs and ready to be unloaded.

I read off names and phone numbers, and Patrick called again those among the "everyone" yet to be notified. After several calls, everyone knew.

At nearly 1 p.m., I noticed that we were on Delmas 33, headed west toward The Neighborhood instead of east toward our warehouse.

The Neighborhood is an unexpected patch of land turned into a tent city surrounded by small cement block buildings and a power plant. A twelve-foot opening serves as the entry point from the main road. On January 12, 2010, the earthquake in Haiti destroyed one-third of the houses in Port au Prince. The next day, tent cities mushroomed across the capital. One of the tents in The Neighborhood protected Patrick and his beloved, Gardine, from the elements, and gave them a flimsy place to belong though their foundations had been shaken. Patrick and Gardine eventually found a rental house and moved a few blocks away, but the bonds in the neighborhood remained strong.

Suffering such a tragedy together created a strong relationship among the neighbors, and they became as close as family. Family watches out for each other, so Patrick tries to extend work opportunities whenever possible. We hire ten day-workers to unload all 38,000 pounds of cargo by hand. Each worker receives a US twenty-dollar bill, as many bags of water as needed to stay hydrated in the hot sun, and a Styrofoam container full of rice, beans, and chicken purchased from a street vendor.

"Do you have to pick up some guys?" The guys usually find their own transportation to work.

"Yeah, the guys have these big scissors to cut off the seal and they can't just go around with 'em," Patrick said as if this was a regular occurrence.

The "big scissors" turned out to be the biggest set of box cutters I have ever seen, easily as tall as my four-year-old granddaughter. "Can't just go around with 'em" indeed! The police would surely mistake the giant box cutter–toting workers for car thieves or kidnappers.

Two workers got into the car with the big scissors, and by 1:30 p.m., we finally arrived at the warehouse, two and a half hours after our expected time. I drew a deep breath and made myself smile. *Well, we're here, so let's get this show on the road.* Miss Plucky tries to look on the bright side! My stomach grumbled. *Must have protein in the morning.* I made a mental note. Citrus and coffee were not cutting it, and I felt my nerves getting tetchy.

Love is patient. Patience is love. Jesus, help me show love. Help me be patient.

A tree service operation was working in the way of our container. And by "tree service operation," I mean a large truck with a hook on a boom and a man with a machete. It took a while to convince machete man to move his vehicle, but by 2:15 p.m., the container was in its place and ready to be unloaded. Patrick took the massive scissors, cut the seal, and opened the container doors.

Unloading Patience

I rejoiced as the first boxes came off the container. Finally! I had tried to be easygoing about the delays, and I was so happy that we still had three and a half hours before sunset. We could do this! This patience thing was paying off. I could see that the reward of living patient love was things going smoothly! I could have hugged all ten day-workers, Patrick, and the machete man.

I rejoiced too soon. A hiccup revealed itself almost immediately. Practicing patience, I wanted to let Patrick be in charge. This was his job, after all. He had done this umpteen times before. But I noticed the labels on the boxes said things like "St. Vincent de Paul," "Redeemer Church," and "Sisters of Charity," organizations I distinctly remembered not calling out to Patrick in the car. I looked at the container number, TGHU-5471 . . . Wait! Mediterranean Shipping Company had shipped the April container; hence the container number should start with MSC, not TGHU.

This was the wrong container. We had the wrong distribution list. We had called the wrong people to pick up their supplies. The wrong people were at that very minute on their way to do just that. It was Patrick's job to know which container we were unloading.

So many thoughts ricocheted through my melting head.

The containers are as big as train cars, forty feet long, eight and a half feet high, and eight feet wide. The laborious process of unloading the container is made more strenuous by lugging everything, box by box, up an incline to the chapel-turned-warehouse. However, when we call people who run the organizations on the list, many of them come to receive their boxes as they are coming off the container.

Yet the wrong people were coming for their stuff.

My lips straightened and my jaw tightened. *Patience, Kim, patience,* whispered the voice in my head. I took a deep breath as I noticed my fingers drumming on the container's side—aggravation bristled as I focused on trying not to fire or throttle my employee. If there was a cartoon bubble over my head, you could have roasted marshmallows in the flames.

"Could this be the June container, not the April container?" Patrick said, innocent as a lamb. *What! Really! Lord, I know that I am praying for patience, but really?* I could have flown into Haiti tomorrow and avoided this challenge. The container could have been released by customs last week before I arrived. Yet here we stand—me on the brink of exploding, and Patrick nonchalant.

"We have to call everybody on both lists," I said, as nicely as possible through gritted teeth. *Jesus, help me. Please!* My tank of human patience was running on fumes, and I needed a filling of divine strength. I knew this fiasco reflected poorly on Rays of Hope, and on me too. Many of the folks we called on the wrong list would have rented trucks, hired day workers, and would start arriving at any minute. They will be frustrated, even aggravated, by this mix-up.

I breathed in and out. My stomach rumbled, reminding me that I hadn't eaten in hours. I could buy some street food, but I pictured the hanging raw chicken, buzzing with flies, and decided a foodborne illness wouldn't improve my patience. The right distribution list had to be found, and fast, so that we could call the correct recipients of this shipment.

"Where's Patrick?" I asked, suddenly noticing he'd vanished again. I felt a little bit faint.

"Patrick *pa la*," one of the guys said in Creole. (Haitian Creole is the language of 90–95% of Haitians. The language developed when African slaves decided to revolt against their French owners and needed to communicate with each other without being understood by the slave owners. It is a mix of French, Spanish, and a couple of West African languages.)

I tried a couple words to find out where he was. *"Pa la?* Not here?"

"Toilette?" No.

"Dlo?" Did he go to get water? No.

I slumped against the container and prayed some more.

After about half an hour, Patrick reappeared, with a printout of the distribution list.

He did it! I knew he would! I exhaled a bit. *Patient love.*

I tried to infuse my voice with goodwill and tolerance as I recommended that Patrick first call those from the wrong list. Some of them had already shown up and left, but perhaps if we acted fast, we could save a trip for others.

"That's what I'm doin'," he softly muttered. "That's what I'm doin'." *Don't micromanage. Let Patrick do it. Stop talking.*

Apparently, Patrick was getting as frustrated with me as I was with him. I realized that my sighs were louder than I thought and my face was not smiling but showing exasperation.

It was 4:49 p.m. and we were burning daylight. I began to hustle a bit more in my efforts to aid the unloading process.

"My phone's losin' charge," Patrick said, as he walked away from the container and toward the car. "I'm gonna charge it up."

"How are the phone calls going?" *Breathe. Patience.*

"Well, the list I have is not the right distribution list."

What?! "So, do you have the right distribution list?" *The one sent to you seven months ago when the container left Rays of Hope's dock. The one that has been sent to you repeatedly since?* Now we need a third list? There surely wasn't enough patience in the world to keep me from screaming, but by some miracle, I stifled my anger.

"I am going to go print it." *Patience. Love is patient.* Patrick was still learning. I was still learning. We were all trying to do it the right way.

I grunted as I lugged boxes off the container and snagged my skirt on an old chair inexplicably sitting in the way. When Patrick returned in half an hour, we were still unloading.

"You broke the chair?" Patrick asked.

"It was me or the chair," I said. "I won."

The good news was that no one else from the wrong list turned up. The bad news was, just forty minutes remained before total darkness. Patrick instructed the guys to start putting everything into the warehouse. Thirty-eight thousand pounds of boxes, tubs, pails, and crates spread over the pavement now had to be picked up again, carried up the incline, and put into the warehouse.

By 6 p.m., the gentle hum and loud roar of generators started to fill the air. It was as black as tar out there, and we were still moving boxes and crates. I remembered the flashlight app on my phone. Then we could move boxes by a little tiny light instead of no light at all.

"Kim! Come here!" I heard Patrick call to me out of the inky sky. My phone read 6:20 p.m.

"Can't you come here?" My voice was no longer infused with tolerance, but with something sour.

"I'm looking at somethin'," he called back. *Oh yes, that explains it. Of course, I need to go there. Patience!*

I daydreamed about throttling him with my bare hands and stepped gingerly through the dark to the guesthouse one hundred feet away. The lights from the generator assaulted my eyes as I beheld Patrick, smiling, holding a plate full of chicken, rice and beans, and fruit. On his last vanishing act, he had arranged for a meal for me. I smiled back at him, sincerely this time, and slid gratefully into a chair to eat.

An hour later, Patrick appeared and told me he finished all of the paperwork. When we pulled out of the compound into the noisy, congested, smoky street, I felt euphoric. Something in me had feared we would never untangle ourselves from the container mix-up, and I'd have to live out my days on the dock, suppressing wrath.

Things looked brighter now, having been fed, with the container unloaded into the warehouse, and leaving—especially leaving.

"Kim, I'm starving. We should get something to eat, then drive to Borel."

"Borel? But Borel is three hours away! We can't possibly still be going to Borel."

"That was the plan! Oh, and I have someone picking up stuff from the warehouse at 7 a.m.," he said, swerving to avoid a crater in the road. "We'll have to leave Borel by 4 a.m."

I know I asked for it, but even patience has its limits. I insisted that the three-hour drive just to sleep a few hours and hit the road again wasn't worth it. So, we drove back to Notre Maison, where Patrick ate and we made a plan for the next day.

It was 11 p.m. when I showered off layers of sweat and grime. As the ice-cold water dribbled on my shoulders, I wondered why I thought it was a good idea to pray for patience. As it turned out, patience is a much more powerful word than I thought. I dried off with a scratchy rag of a towel and climbed into bed.

"Help me, Jesus. Thank you for saving me today, from myself, from doing something I'd regret. Help me understand patience better. Help me understand love." Tomorrow was another day, and another chance to live love.

As I drifted off, scenes from the hard hours that had passed flitted through my mind and I had a revelation. Patrick knew patient love; he lived it all day long. He had never been flustered, had never yelled or snapped. Patrick was present, aware, unwavering. I was so consumed in this quest to discover the meaning of patient love, I didn't see it demonstrated through my self-indulgent haze. Now that the fog had lifted, it became so clear. Patrick lived such patient love. It was part of his being, woven in the fabric of his soul. My naked soul would have to deliberately work on living love that is patient. Maybe if I had recognized this sooner, I would have learned the meaning of patient love while there was still daylight. I had one last conscious thought: *Patience, I desire you . . . sort of.*

People Aren't Interruptions

Haiti is a gifted professor. Haitian culture schools my patience, or at least my previous understanding of patience. Before this year of living love, I thought that waiting without complaining was patience, that not expecting everyone to be in an American hurry was *extra* patience. And I thought not caving in to frustration during a traffic jam in a city of nearly two million people—with infrastructure for only forty thousand people—was top-drawer, gold-medal, long-suffering patience. But I am pretty sure I had it wrong.

That day with Patrick at the warehouse revealed something to me: the essence of patience is being present in the moment. I had been entirely *absent* from the moment, racing ahead in my mind, worried about the consequences of Patrick's mistakes. Being in the moment is *not* thinking ahead about that long to-do list or the mass of emails that need to be returned. It means being more concerned with showing love to a slow checkout clerk at the grocery store than getting home after a grueling day. It means living love in the minute, with a human being, not an obstacle to my plans.

Patient love realizes that people are more important than agendas. Everything else will wait, can wait. Had I practiced being in the moment with Patrick, I would have been calmer, more accepting, less put out, less perturbed.

By being present in the moment, body and soul, mind and spirit, the moment takes on a new reality. A fullness. A wholeness. Senses heighten, minds open, and hearts engage.

Mother to child.

Husband to wife.

Friend to friend.

Stranger to stranger.

Love is present in the moment while patient love embraces and encircles the moment. It listens, sees, feels, and, because of that, it waits. Patient love waits, knowing that this is the most important moment of your life. What is in the past stays there. What is ahead isn't here yet. Nothing else matters besides right here, right now.

In understanding love that is patient, I also understand that, first, it is not natural for me. Second, it is going to take a lot of work and a whole lot of focus to just be in the moment and not be distracted by the thousands of interruptions vying for my attention. This love is not going to be a one-day, follow the directions and put the Ikea coffee table together kind of learning. It will be more like learning how to surf in crazy high waves with great white sharks waiting for their dinner to take a nosedive. Ignoring the squirrel, the shiny object, and the vibrating cell phone takes some time.

It all sounds right, but what is the reality? What does practicing patient love look like to a type A raised by a type A+? It looks like focusing on focusing, intentionally putting on blinders, tuning out all other sounds, having a gold medal-worthy stare-down contest with the moment. Think of that tracking device that we all carry around in our pockets and purses—you know, the one that sounds like wind chimes, an alien spacecraft, or the first bar of a favorite song? The one that gets all of our attention? We can be midsentence and if that thing makes a sound, the whole world stops while our eyes immediately move to look at the screen. Maybe patient love means finding the off button.

Lord Jesus, I think of all of the times that I have not shown patient love, nodding my head as if I was listening while my mind was already on the next task. Lord, help me to live in the moment. Help me to have patient love. I desire patience, patience that waits, patient love—and this time, I really mean it.

CHAPTER 2

LOVE IS KIND

KIND. THIS ONE SHOULD BE easy. I do acts of kindness every day. I smile and wave at people I pass on the sidewalk. I offer a coworker a cup of coffee if I am going to get one myself. I open a door, give a compliment, share some mints, and feed the birds. I volunteer, give money, and help promote great causes.

As far back as I can remember, my parents taught me how to be kind, particularly after I got caught doing something unkind. Banished to my bedroom, instructed to think about the tragedy of my actions and how my behavior would need to change in the future, I mostly spent the time counting the flowers on my wallpaper.

Notebooks could be filled with my lessons learned in solitary confinement. Hitting my brother is unkind. Avoiding my brother when one of us is in a bad mood is kind. Calling someone stupid is unkind. Calling someone pretty is kind. Taking the last of the cake is unkind. Sharing the cake is kind. Holding a puppy gently is kind. Dropping a puppy is unkind. (I was only four and it truly was an accident. Prince had very sharp teeth.)

A while back, a great book started a movement, a challenge. All over the world, people were caught doing random acts of kindness. What an incredible, world-changing concept! Once people began practicing kindness, scoping out ways to show more of it became a part-time job. The world started paying for the hamburgers of strangers, toll booth charges of truckers, and cappuccinos for coffee lovers.

I hopped right on that random acts of kindness train. I imagined the amazement and gratitude of the person behind me at the Starbucks drive-through. Pulling up to the window, they would hear, "Your bill is paid." Spending six bucks to make someone's day, absolutely. But seeing a minivan full of baseball jerseys at Dog n Suds kept my random dollars in my kindness wallet.

While coaching volleyball, I tossed the concept out to my team and they came up with a list of deed ideas, enjoyable, extreme, and exhausting, that took up a whole page in my playbook. Because we all agreed that unexpectedly doing something for someone who hates doing it earned the highest number of kindness points, we went to a local diner to clean the bathrooms. We were not just playing the random acts game; we were in it to win it.

The hostess, puzzled by our offer, flagged down the big boss. Skip the dining room manager; the head honcho had to hear this one.

"You want to do what?"

"We want to clean your bathrooms." Putting all of our smiles end to end would have nearly encircled the globe.

"We have a service for that."

"Sure, but we thought we could give them a break."

"But that is how they make a living."

Totally deflated but not defeated, our team captain asked, "What can we do?"

"You are welcome to get a table and order some food. This is a restaurant."

Now defeated.

My team concluded that scrubbing porcelain ranked up there with a whole practice of just running sprints. Who would turn down toilet cleaners? In hindsight, it was obviously not the best choice from our extensive list. Cleaning the bathroom in someone's home would have been good. Cleaning the bathrooms in my home would have been great. I don't remember that being on our list.

We didn't give up on kindness. Looking for opportunities, we surprised our opponents with treats, helped put away their equipment, and made brownies for the officials. It was so fun to see the grins triggered by our unexpected kindnesses. The brownies may have been given with a hint of desire to grease the referee's whistle, but were still kind.

After a while, school, sports, and family demands took away time from kind acts. I haven't had Starbucks myself in a long time, let alone buying a cup for someone else.

At the beginning of this love-is-kind adventure, I assumed that figuring it out in Haiti shouldn't take long. Kindness seemed pretty clear. I was just kind in Creole instead of English. Still, I remembered shoveling through a mountain to uncover patient love and realized I wasn't necessarily a quick learner.

In late February of 2014, I arrived with a big bag of peanut M&Ms. I hoped that the sweetness of the candy might sweeten Patrick's recollection of my frustration during "patient" month. Bringing candy, his favorite candy, was kind. Having a little something for everyone in Patrick's family was really kind. Kind is easy.

Keeping kindness on my mind, I helped with dishes at the end of each meal, assisting Mimose, chief cook and bottle washer at the orphanage. Because of a former embarrassing situation, I made sure that she got paid the same whether I helped or not to avoid a rerun of "Kindness at the Diner." I was the last in line for dinner and the first one to be ready to get on the bus. I spent more time with the kids, bought Patrick lunch way before lunchtime, and even tipped the waiter an American 20 percent rather than the Haitian 10 percent. Love is kind.

Kindness Goes to the Zoo

The group that came to Haiti with me wanted to take some of the kids who lived at Notre Maison to the zoo. The zoo, meaning a small fenced-in area at Baptist Haiti Mission that housed a peacock, a couple of goats, rabbits, guinea pigs, a snake or two, an iguana, and a categorically crazy monkey. The only zoo in a country one and a half times the size of Massachusetts with nearly double its population.

I was briefly hesitant, but kindness took over my fear of losing someone and I made arrangements.

Many of the children, from toddlers to late teens, had been left as infants on the stairs at General Hospital, the largest public medical center in the capital. They were abandoned because it is hard to raise a completely healthy child in the poorest country in the western hemisphere, and raising a child with challenges is nearly impossible. Gertrude, the empress of Notre Maison, started visiting the children who were placed together in a small room and pretty much left to fend for themselves. She would bring food, love the babies, and cry when she had to go, knowing that their chances of survival were slim to none. So she figured out a way to rent a big house and bring the children home. Home to Notre Maison, Our House. Because Gertrude knows love that is kind.

The kids who could go to school attended while the others stayed behind the concrete-block wall that surrounded their two-story dwelling. It was incredibly kind that the people visiting Haiti with me, new to this land, were so loving, kind, and willing to spend their time and money giving children they just met the best day of their lives.

A ride on a bus was thrill number one. Going out somewhere, anywhere, was such a rare treat. Giddy with excitement, some of the kids waved at everyone we passed, others laughed for no reason at all, and a few rocked in their padded seats giggling over every bump and dip in the road. If all we did was go for a bus tour around the block, each child would have felt like it had been a trip to Disney World, a memory that would last as long as a memory can last. With the streets in Haiti like they are and the traffic like it is, it would not surprise me if Walt visited Port au Prince to get his inspiration for Mr. Toad's Wild Ride, so it was kind of a Haitian version of a Disney experience.

Each person in my group was assigned a child. With one-on-one attention, there was little room for error. But this was Haiti, and Haiti doesn't need much room.

With kindness exuding from every pore of my being, I smiled as the bus stopped at Epidore, Haiti's answer to fast food offering burgers, fries, and other greasy dishes. Baked goods and Haitian entrees are also on the menu, but the bond between kids and deep fryers is strong worldwide.

The spectacle compelled stares. A group of obvious foreigners walked hand in hand with children rarely seen, including some who walked a little funny, some who looked a little different. All had been left outside of a hospital and were expected to never be spotted again, certainly not walking into a restaurant.

Leaving the walls was rare; riding a bus, rarer yet; eating in a restaurant, probably a first for most if not all of the children.

I gave everyone the rundown on what to do. "You go there to order and pay for your food, then take your receipt over there where they will use a fingernail to make a line on the paper, then go down there to wait for your food."

Somehow through the hustle and bustle at the peak of the lunch hour, getting papers, getting food, and finding tables, everyone made it into the right lines and arrived back at our saved places. Chicken strips and French fries got the most orders with pizza not far behind.

Junior, one of the older residents, is such a special guy. The gatekeeper. Without fail, anytime anyone comes into or goes out of the gated walls, Junior is there holding the sliding metal door with a smile as infectious as Cameron Diaz's, giving a big thumbs-up greeting, or a big thumbs-up farewell. Nineteen years old, just over five feet tall, Junior's words are few, but his joy is abundant.

After Junior had quickly devoured round one, Dave and Angie, the lovely couple who were Junior's tag team, decided he might want some more. Dave finished with the pay-and-get-your-receipt line, got the mark, and headed to pick up more chicken and French fries while Angie waited at the table with Junior.

I was preoccupied with keeping an eye on twenty adults and twenty kids all at the same time when I heard a commotion. Loud voices shouted loud Creole words as a man grabbed my arm and led me over to a large potted tree. I had seen trees before, so it took a minute to understand the urgency of seeing another. The only thing unique about this one was it had a nineteen-year-old giving a big thumbs-up standing in front of it. The voices got louder as more people joined the chorus. I was alarmed for my whole group, knowing there must be something unsavory happening. The man who had a hold of me directed my attention to the ground. There was something brown on the floor as though someone had spilled chocolate pudding. It was then that I noticed Junior's pants on the ground next to and partially in the pile of, oh yes, that brown stuff. He wasn't just standing in front of the planter; he was backing up as though hoping to fertilize the tree. I understood right away how this scene might disrupt someone's meal.

Claudy, a dear friend who was working with us as a translator, came rushing over. He gently put one hand on Junior's shoulder and used the other to snatch Junior's pants, then walked him to the men's room.

People were still yelling as Junior marched away, shouting for me to clean it up, I guessed. Poop and vomit are not my things. Not that they are anyone's things, but I would just be adding to the foul-smelling pile of chocolate cake batter. (I can't even call it what it is without heaving a little.) Fortunately, some kind Epidor employee slid in for the rescue with a mop and bucket.

Working on damage control, I silently listed the facts on the legal pad in my head.

1. Poor Junior is sick.
2. We do not have extra pants.
3. We have one bus for all of us.
4. There is no way that I can ride in what had seemed like a good-sized bus but that my gag reflex is remembering now as a small van, and keep my lunch at the same time.
5. It's pretty unkind to worry more about the smell than how Junior feels. That's not love.

6. I am the leader, an adult; I am supposed to solve all issues promptly.
7. I am already on number seven and not even close to a solution.

Just then, I saw Claudy and sheepish Junior, pants on, walking toward me. Knowing there was no way that Claudy, bless his soul, could have scrubbed the stink out of Junior's trousers, I stopped breathing through my nose and wondered if that was unkind.

"Junior is sick." Claudy made the transition from translator to doctor rather quickly. "We have to take him home."

The kids already had a pretty special day and, for the most part, were still munching on desserts, unfazed by the noise, unrest, or odor.

Claudy then made the kindest offer in the history of all offers since the beginning of time. He said that he would get Junior home so that the others could still go to the zoo.

Relieved that I could keep my stomach from adding to the hysteria, I stepped outside with Claudy to flag down a moto. Motos are motorcycles not much bigger than the one my brother took on trails when he was a freshman in high school. In Haiti, my brother's bike would taxi as many as five people.

The first guy we flagged down took one whiff of Junior and said, "Hasta la vista, baby."

Several minutes passed and still no takers.

"Offer more money."

"How much?"

Right then, I would have given every last penny and gourde I had. "Whatever you think."

Claudy started negotiating with drivers and was finally able to make it worth someone's trouble.

As Junior climbed on the back of the 125cc Haojin, Claudy asked for five hundred gourdes, less than five dollars, then slid on, sandwiching Junior between himself and the driver. I wondered how much The Terminator would have charged had his smeller been working.

The good news is Junior was on cloud nine. I found out that his biggest dream was to hitch a ride on a motorcycle. Right then, he was the happiest, smelliest guy in the world.

Five dollars barely buys a Happy Meal, but that day five dollars bought a way home for Junior, a busload of happy kids, and a very relieved team leader. So kind, Claudy. Like love.

Kindness Takes Time

I was pretty disappointed in myself for thinking I knew kindness, acted kindly, and was generally kind, but then didn't *think* kindly. I didn't want to be very close to Junior for one minute, and definitely not for a full trip back to Noitre Maison. Here I thought I was living it, breathing it, being it—and then I totally blew it when the going got tough. Either I was not kind, so I did not love, or I completely missed the meaning of love that is kind.

I knew then that this was not going to be a cakewalk after all. I started doubting myself and wondered if I really would figure out love that is kind.

The next day, I met Christopher.

Christopher was just three weeks old. I found him amidst the sea of institutional cribs in the lower level of Sisters of Charity Home for Sick Children, an incredible sanctuary in the center of a neighborhood devastated by decades of poverty and the ravages of the earthquake. His pink terry cloth sleeper hid the tape securing an IV inserted by one of the compassionate members of Mother Teresa's order. Miniature fingers with miniature fingernails poked out of his sleeves. His delicate features, in exact proportion, were the kind modeled in paintings by the masters. His eyelashes were as long as if they had been purchased. Petite brows crowned his face. His skin, the color of caramel cooked just a bit too long, had the feel of expensive silk. Jet black hair covered his scalp but was no longer than the nearly translucent peach fuzz on his cheeks. A clear plastic tube separated the brownish-pink heart that was his mouth from his glossy, dark chocolate eyes. Two nearly invisible prongs placed gently in his tiny nostrils were allowing oxygen to feed his lungs. He looked so relaxed, sprawled out on his back, almost melting into the mattress. He was peaceful, beautiful, and perfect.

I reached down to hold his hand, and I noticed a woman standing at the end of his crib. She was something less than five feet tall with a very slight frame. Her coarse hair was pulled back into a short ponytail. Sadness hovered over her, making the yellow happy faces on her short-sleeved cotton dress look out of place. She had Christopher's dark eyes—or he had hers. Her face was a dichotomy, somehow both worn and weathered from what I imagined to be working for years in the hot Haiti sun and soft and lovely like a young, innocent schoolgirl who doesn't yet know how pretty she is.

As the morning went by, Nathalie and Christopher's story unfolded.

Christopher's first breath was on the dirt floor of Nathalie's one-room home. His mother, Nathalie's only child, died shortly after giving birth. Nathalie thought Christopher's inability to keep milk in his stomach was because it was not his mother's. She hoped his body would adapt quickly. As days went by, Christopher became less and less interested in the bottle and more and more intent on sleeping. Nathalie held Christopher close on the several mile walk to the Sisters. By the time Christopher arrived, he was not only lethargic but his breathing was labored. The Sisters found Christopher a donated sleeper likely worn by a treasured baby girl born in a clean hospital with the best medical care available somewhere in the United States. An empty crib with a clean sheet welcomed him. A clean place on the floor welcomed his grandmother.

Dehydration called for the IV and shallow breathing prompted the oxygen. With no more sophisticated equipment than a stethoscope, the best guess was Christopher had an abdominal obstruction.

At first, Nathalie was afraid to touch her grandson when there were intimidating tubes and needles everywhere. After I held Christopher's hand for a bit, she reached out and did the same.

As the number of passing minutes grew, so did our bond, the bond that comes naturally, woman to woman, mom to mom, grandma to grandma. We held each other, never letting go of her grandson's tiny hands.

I have felt Nathalie's pain. I ran into an emergency room to see my four-year-old daughter trapped in a spiderweb of tubes, each doing something to stop her seizure. My tears added to those of my son and daughter-in-law while they were cuddling their son for the two and a half hours of his life. I crawled into the oxygen tent that was helping my five-month-old son survive a potentially terminal virus. Eight months pregnant, I slept in a chair in an intensive care unit the night the doctor told us our four-year-old daughter might never walk or talk again.

Like Nathalie, I have cried, prayed, and pleaded for God's mercy. Like Nathalie, I know anguish, pain, and grief. Like Nathalie, my gut ached, my head swam, and my heart broke.

Unlike Nathalie, I have a modern hospital down the street, my doctor's office on speed dial, and a Walgreens within walking distance. Unlike Nathalie, I have clean water at the turn of a faucet, plenty of food in my refrigerator, and carpeting on my floors. Unlike Nathalie, I was never without family in a hospital, friends able to help, or funds to pay the costs. And, unlike Nathalie, I did not watch my only child die.

At one point during the day, Christopher stopped breathing and so did we. In a panic, we somehow discovered a kink in his oxygen tube. As soon as we straightened the tube, we all breathed again.

Four hours in, it was clear that Christopher's only hope was surgery at one of the handful of hospitals in this city with more than two million residents.

In my hometown, experienced paramedics would come with a portable oxygen tank and watch him closely while transporting him in an ambulance. In Nathalie's hometown, finding a paramedic or an ambulance is like finding buried treasure on an island. I soon discovered that finding a portable oxygen tank in Nathalie's hometown was like finding buried treasure in an ocean.

I called everyone I could think of in Port au Prince who might know where to find a portable oxygen tank. Most could not even recommend a place to go for one; some drove to look for one; nobody could find one.

Without surgery, Christopher would die. Without oxygen, Christopher would die. His poor grandma had to make the call.

The closest hospital was put on alert that Christopher would soon be arriving. A driver pulled up to the nearest exit, keeping the engine running. When the van was in place, one sister grabbed Christopher's IV bag while another scooped him into her arms, pulling the oxygen away from his face. In a blur of white habits, the sisters and Christopher disappeared.

I turned back to the crib and saw Nathalie.

I said, "Ali, ali! Go, go!"

My eyes followed Nathalie's tears and pointing finger to her bare feet. She knew she would not be allowed in the hospital without shoes. I quickly kicked off my sandals and gave them to Nathalie. I grabbed her by the hand, pulling her out into the street just as the van door was closing. Nathalie ran, grabbed the handle, and jumped in.

It pains me to say that Nathalie lost her precious grandson that day. How I wish this story had a happy ending. If Christopher was born where my grandchildren were, he would have had surgery. In a few years, he would be having pirate adventures, playing with trucks, and finding frogs. He would be celebrating birthdays, learning how to ride a bike, and constructing a fort out of sticks. In a few more years, he would be graduating from high school, then college, maybe followed by medical school where he could learn how to help other Christophers.

Same earth, different world.

Kind love became so obvious that day. Kind love is giving of yourself without expecting anything in return. Not anything. Not a thank-you, not a reciprocal act, not a nod of acknowledgment. Kind love is giving, helping, sharing when you know that it is impossible to get something in return. I thought about that. I started thinking about the times when I complained that I didn't even get a thank-you. Or when I helped someone move, attended their daughter's wedding, brought them food when they were sick, and then wondered where they were with my daughter's wedding gift. I have done lots of kind things. I have not shown kind love.

First laser-focused patient love and now no-expectation kind love. Shouldn't love be easy, natural?

I gave Nathalie my sandals knowing that I would never see them or her again. I showed kind love before I truly understood it. I did not consider my own bare feet for even a millisecond. I would go shoeless for the rest of my life if it meant that Nathalie could hold Christopher. Love is kind, period. Doing kind, living kind, giving kind. Love gives the shirt off your back, a motorcycle ride home, and the sandals off your feet. Just because love is kind.

Nathalie opened her heart and shared her only grandson during what was likely the hardest time of her life. I will never forget her kindness, and I will never stop loving Christopher. I had no thought about receiving something back, but Nathalie gave me so much more than a pair of shoes.

Lord, help me look for so many opportunities to practice kind love that it becomes part of my nature and expectations become just a vague memory.

CHAPTER 3

LOVE DOES NOT ENVY

Envy. Now there is a word.

Love is patient, and patience is nice. Love is kind; kindness is good. Love does not envy; envy sounds terrible no matter how you say it. It's insidious, unscrupulous, shady. Unlike envy, jealousy is hanging on tight to what is already yours. God is a jealous God. Exodus, Numbers, and Deuteronomy all tell us so. He wants us and he wants us to have no other god. Envy, on the other hand, is resentment and covetousness over someone's success, wealth, relationship, beauty, talent. It wants something that someone else has and isn't happy that someone else has it. It is what makes a good story villain like the Black Swan, Gaston, or the Wicked Witch of the West. Envy makes a good thief; the Grinch stole Christmas, Ursula pillaged a voice, and Plankton does all kinds of dastardly deeds to plunder a sandwich recipe. Envy can even lead to murder. Murder! Darth Vader, Voldemort, Scar. Not just in fiction, real people have real envy. Cain wanted to be God's favorite. David desired someone else's wife. Ahab's envy led Jezebel to get a guy killed over a vineyard.

Of course, love doesn't envy. Envy is evil; it is one of the seven deadly sins right up there with greed, gluttony, and lust. Why even mention it? It would be like saying, "Love does not hand out poisoned apples" or "Love does not steal spotted puppies to make coats." It seems so obvious yet somehow important enough to be one of just a dozen words used in 1 Corinthians to describe what love is and what love is not.

For years I was told that everyone had a special gift, and I wondered where my present was hiding. I learned what it wasn't, sometimes in challenging ways. When my cousins and I got to the talent portion of the beauty contest in our grandparents' living room, one skill I lacked became painfully apparent. First, ten-year-old Mary Jo sang about "Amazing Grace" that saved a "wrench" and had my grandma smiling from ear to ear. "Oh, Mary, you have such a beautiful voice." Next, Cheri, then five and always full of bubbly joy, took the stage with her rendition of "Paper Roses." Grandma burst with pride, taking in every note of the angelic rendition. "Oh, Cheri, you have such a beautiful voice." I was so excited to step on the kitchen-rug-turned-performance-hall and hear those same words from the person whose opinion I respected the most, who was undoubtedly honest and not at all biased. The walls vibrated with pleasure as I passionately belted out every verse of "King of the Road"; at that moment, I was a man of means by no means. My ears were ready to hear the fantastic critique of my outstanding presentation. And then Grandma said, "Oh, Kim, maybe you can dance."

Hard as it was to hear, my grandma knew her stuff. Cheri and Mary went on to perform on stages all over the state, including my grandparents' Baptist church. I went on to perform for the water stream in the shower. No doubt, I was envious.

So why envy? I wasn't sure that I would figure this one out, but God has his ways.

Envy Comes Naturally

Because of my determination, or what some might call stubbornness (I don't think that one is in the Love Chapter), I kept envy on my mind. I looked for it. I tried to uncover it. I sought it out.

I thought I found it in Haiti in March 2014.

Haitians have a perception that if your skin is light, you are rich. One round-trip flight from Grand Rapids, Michigan, to Port au Prince costs more than most Haitians make in a year. Sometimes I return home and throw away tomatoes that have wilted in my refrigerator while I was wilting under the Haitian sun. My carry-on suitcase can hold some of my Haitian friends' entire wardrobes. So, yes, when wallets are as empty as stomachs and closets, someone who flies on a plane, throws away food, and has as many T-shirts as a small boutique is rich. It makes sense that I would find envy.

Because the coach seats oversold, I bumped to first class, a privilege offered to frequent fliers. I had tomato juice before the plane began to taxi. Once we were in the air, a pleasant steward handed me a hot wet towel to wash my hands before delivering a ramekin of toasted mixed nuts. The steward offered wine with lunch that included chicken parmesan over pasta and a side salad with a plump, non-wilted cherry tomato. I could smell the cookies baking when they took away my tray. Soon I was navigating the delightfully messy confection oozing with melted chocolate. I leaned back in my reclining seat, pushed a button that lifted my feet in the air, covered up with the complimentary blanket, and watched a movie on my own personal screen using earbuds, again complimentary. I wondered if the people behind the blue curtain with their half can of Coke and a small bag of pretzels were envious.

As soon as I made it to baggage claim, the requests began. Most were nonverbal since the Creole-speaking porters assumed the majority of visitors did not speak their language. Wide-eyed, first-time visitors just stared as the seemingly chaotic scene unfolded. Guys in airport-logoed, button-down, navy-blue shirts grabbed at bags as fearful shouts of "no, thank you" came from people who had most likely been warned to hang on to their bags because "someone might run off with them!" Since this was not my first visit, I knew that these guys were just trying to make a couple of bucks to feed themselves and probably their families. No one planned on hopping the fence with a bag full of some stranger's three-ounce bottles of toiletries and some used unmentionables. Some of these blue-shirted men had become my friends over the years, so my "no, thank yous" were few and far between.

"Jordan! Mwen rate ou!"

Jordan said he missed me too.

"Jackson! Como ou ye?"

"Mwen byen. Ou?" Good, and you?

"Pa pi mal, mwen zanmi." Not bad, my friend.

I am always happy to give Jordan or Jackson my small bag to carry and a few dollars for their wallets.

One of my best friends at the airport is one of the happiest people I have ever known. He isn't allowed inside the airport but magically appears as soon as I walk out the door.

Ramy is the only deaf guy hustling for tips at Toussaint Louverture International Airport in Port au Prince. Standing about six feet tall, pretty tall for this country, Ramy grabbed me and hugged me. Then he pointed to his eyes and back at me. "I saw you!" Then he pointed to his heart and back at me. "I love you." Then up to the sky his finger flew. "I've been praying for you."

I made all of the gestures with him and then we hugged again. My suitcase in one hand and his other around my shoulder, Ramy walked me to where Patrick was waiting in a car. He was smiling and pointing the whole time to his eyes, to his heart, to the sky. We hugged a couple more times. I gave him some money, and he put his hands together like a prayer, bowing a bit. "Thank you."

"You are welcome, my friend," I spoke without sound.

Driving away from the airport, I thought about envy, love that does not envy. I felt that with Ramy, love was just happy to see me. No envy, just happiness. I was starting to feel like this trip would lead me to some great envy (or lack thereof) discoveries.

Years ago, I heard an interview with Maury Povich. He said something that I will never forget: "Poviches root for Poviches." He talked about celebrating his siblings' victories, honors, and rewards, not comparing themselves, just truly desiring the best for each other. They didn't envy, they loved, and love does not envy.

This was a little foreign to me, coming from a highly competitive family. "I betcha" was a pretty common phrase in my home, and we "betcha'd" everything. I betcha can't beat me up the stairs. I betcha stop running before I do. I betcha blink first. We had to be the quickest, the smartest, the best. And whoever wasn't the fastest, the brightest, the best, envied the one who was. Opposite of the Poviches, we envied, not loved, at least not at that moment.

Envy traveled outside our house too. There was the prettiest girl, the smartest in the class, the best athlete. But the prettiest girl had smelly armpits, the smartest guy cheated on tests, and the best athlete was just lucky. So we said. But it wasn't true. There was no smelling, cheating, or luck. There was just ugly envy.

After I heard "Poviches root for Poviches," I realized there was a different way.

In looking for envy in Port au Prince, I found that I was complaining about some things I actually envied.

No one ever seems to be in a hurry. We were tooling along (if you can tool along on overcrowded streets in Port au Prince) when Patrick saw a friend coming in the opposite direction. So, of course, we did the ever-so-logical-stop-and-chat in the middle of the street.

"Sak pase!"

"N'ap boule." Cars in front of us, trucks behind us, horns honked, people yelled, none of it mattered. Patrick just smiled and asked his friend what he was up to, and his friend basically said, "Just hangin'," followed by some other unfamiliar words asking about each other's "famni" and which team was going to win the World Cup.

There was a time I would have been nudging Patrick to get moving, but I learned that I have to just roll with it, whatever it is, or "it" will drive me crazy. Eventually, after what seemed like twenty minutes, but was likely just one or two, we started moving again.

Patrick said, "That was a friend of mine."

"That's nice. I wish I had time just to stop and talk to a friend in the middle of the street," I snarked.

"Huh?"

Then it hit me. I really did wish that I had time to just stop and talk to a friend, though maybe on the side rather than the middle of the road. Hmm, envy?

A few minutes later, we drove past the most beautiful woman selling beans on the sidewalk. She had the kind of beauty that could get out of bed in the morning, throw on a burlap sack, and still be asked to compete in the Miss Universe contest. Vidal Sassoon could do my hair while Bobbi Brown applied makeup and the fairy godmother bibbidi bobbidi dressed me, and I still wouldn't look that good. Oh, envy.

We pulled up next to a big black SUV with the name of a large nonprofit organization painted on the passenger side door. Dark tinted windows were rolled all the way up in the hundred-degree heat. I could almost smell the soft leather seats that I knew must be inside the very cool air-conditioned vehicle. I pictured a bank book with some number followed by a lot of zeros. I looked down at the rip in my seat. With the hot sun penetrating our very clear windshield as the heat poured in from the open windows. I was in that moment one with the after-bucket Wicked Witch of the West, drenched and melting. I imagined being one of the people in the fancy truck with third-row seating, remote starter, cup holders, working windshield wipers, over-the-shoulder seat belts, four matching tires, a built-in cooler full of delicious snacks, and a cappuccino/smoothie machine, sitting up high on their piles of money. Man, what I could do for education in Haiti with all of that money! And, boy, what I wouldn't give for a banana mango smoothie. OK, I get it. Envy.

Envy, the ugly green-eyed monster, was everywhere I looked. I had been practicing patient love and no-expectations kind love, and all along envy had me by the throat, killing my love mojo. I had to figure this out because love does not envy.

I needed to get Poviched and be happy for Patrick that he got to say hello to an old friend. I should just admire the woman's beauty, beauty that God created. I should be grateful for the work of the nonprofit organization and for those who gave to it, and I should realize that you can probably get a lot more done if your car isn't always breaking down and you can feel fresh going into the next meeting.

Envy on the Road to Adventure

After finishing a building project in Haiti, my Dominican son, Cristian, and his crew headed home, leaving behind a stake truck that I, along with my good friends Tom and Todd, agreed to drive to the Dominican Republic a few days later. The truck, used by Lighthouse Projects in the Dominican Republic to deliver five-gallon jugs of water, is like an oversized pickup truck with a bench seat in the front and a bed with short walls in the back.

We had sketchy to no cell service and no GPS available, so we pulled out a map. Having had no previous issues at the border, we expected the five-and-a-half-hour trip would be pretty uneventful.

The road between Port au Prince and the Dominican Republic border is among the nicest in the country. Wide, paved, providing a nice, smooth ride. As expected, the hour-and-a-half drive to the border was a dream. After a week of driving in heavily congested traffic and seriously pitted dirt roads, smooth pavement felt like riding on silk.

Talking and laughing, we got to the border before we knew it. You hear a lot of advice when people know that you are crossing the border. "Don't give them your passport." "Don't stop if they try to flag you down." "Just go to the one building for both stamps." "Whatever you do, don't stop before the gate."

Yeah, yeah, this isn't my first rodeo.

In the past, I had only crossed from the Dominican Republic into Haiti, never the other way around, but I was sure it was the same. We always stop at the one main building, and the first window stamps passports leaving the DR. We go down the complex a bit, where passports get stamped to enter Haiti. Just do that in reverse, and we are golden.

A few miles away from the immigration offices, the landscape changes. With the largest lake in Haiti nearby, Lake Azuéi, the view is breathtaking. But although it resembles Lake of the Ozarks, an excellent place for summer homes and family vacations, Lake Azuéi is not a place that people long to go for a holiday. The brackish water is not known for great fishing. Instead, it is known for the monsters that keep people from going into deep waters to fish, crossing the lake in a boat, or building a cottage on its shores. Alligators live in the waters, four hundred of them at last guesstimate. With that many hungry gators, it's not my first choice of places to bring small children and dogs for a picnic. But beautiful all the same.

Things were looking a little different than I remembered approaching the border. The lake flooded over its shores, covering the road on both sides of the gate. To our left, in terrain resembling the Forbidden Zone from *Planet of the Apes*, a school was partially underwater. Dead trees, big rocks, and terra-cotta dirt covered the inclining ground.

We were paying more attention to the scenery than the road, and so the three of us were shocked when my computer flew off my lap, hitting the ceiling along with my body and part of Todd's. It took us a minute to realize the beautiful, smooth road had a huge pothole. I landed safely, as did my computer, but Todd somehow got a big gash in his knee. The steering wheel kept Tom safe.

Not envious one bit of Todd's painful-looking injury, because love does not envy, I just said, "Well, that will leave a scar."

Big trucks with big loads parked front to back, packed tour buses filled mostly with Haitians going to buy clothes or other items to vend, several motos, and a handful of passenger vehicles crowded the area. Scores of pedestrians lined the road. Some tried to jump into the back of our truck, and injured Todd volunteered to ride in the bed to save our tools. On the passenger side of the road sat a small temporary building like the trailers used on construction sites.

A stone's throw from the entryway, as we followed closely behind one of the tour buses, men started charging our truck. As they hit the sides, yelling at us, we kept our eyes and the wheels pointing forward.

Driving through half a mile of the river that had taken over the street, we reached the gate and then pushed through some more river

on the other side. Also underwater was the building that held the passport stampers when I crossed before. Tom parked as there was no sig-
nage letting us know where to go.

The three of us stood outside, discussing our next move, when a
young Dominican man approached.

"Do you know what you are doing?"

"No idea."

"Do you have your paperwork?"

"What paperwork?"

"From the Haitian side."

We were supposed to stop at the little trailer. A sign would have
been nice. Men hitting our truck and yelling was the sign's substitute.
I must have missed that in the travel blogs.

Our new friend, Luis, told us we had to go back but couldn't take
the truck. Luis helped negotiate a price for three motorcycle drivers to
take us back through the river. Tom stayed with the vehicle to guard
its cargo.

Going back through the river, this time so close to the ground, gave
a better appreciation of the water's depth. I had to lift my feet as high
as possible while keeping my balance, and my driver was not amused
when I had to grab him to catch myself. Some bikes with lower engines
stalled and needed to be pushed across. I prayed for a high engine. I
did not envy the low-engine riders.

As we ended our ride in the gaggle of people, Luis asked for the
three passports. "Just give them to me and some money."

I know that love always trusts (because I have read ahead), but that
is not a chapter I had lived yet, so trust was not my first thought.
"We'll go with you."

"No."

We argued a bit and then followed him in.

Finally, at the front of the line, the customs agent just wanted
money, something you don't give a customs agent when flying out of
the country. I got the price down a bit, our passports got stamped, and
we hopped back on the motorcycles for another hydrofoil ride.

Tom, sitting on top of the truck with a big hammer, was relieved to see us, nervous about having to defend the booty longer than the forty-five minutes we were already gone. Thinking Todd and I had the worst of it, I didn't envy Tom either.

I tried to pay our drivers the agreed-upon amount, but they decided it wasn't enough. Having been taken advantage of a time or two, I knew better than to give in, leaving three men, much larger than me, pretty angry.

Todd and I took our passports and some more money to the officials on this side of the border. Getting our stamps into the Dominican Republic was a breeze. Tom took the wheel, he and I in the cab. Todd jumped in the back for security, then so did Luis. Maybe he just needed a ride.

As we drove slowly down the dirt road connecting the Dominican customs office with the rest of the country, Todd started yelling, "Go! Go faster."

Because the dirt and stones were loose underneath us, Tom maintained our speed.

"Tom! Go! Go faster!"

Tom sped up a bit but was concerned about losing the guys in the back.

"Go! Go! Go! Go. Faster. Now!"

It was then that we noticed the three men who felt cheated by the prearranged fee on our tail. Rocks the size of grapefruit pummeled the truck, thrown by the motorcycle gang's recruits. Tom put the gas pedal to the floor, fishtailing a little, straightened again, and did not let up, taking the first curve at breakneck speed. Like a video game driver, Tom focused only on the road. Right then, I wished it was a video game. If you hit a tree, you just start over again.

Maintaining speed, Tom maneuvered the twists and turns like Mario Andretti. Hell's Angels were in relentless pursuit, sometimes coming alongside the vehicle to try to force Tom to the side of the road, other times so close to the rear bumper that if we stopped, there would be a whole bunch of us in the front seat.

After a few miles, they gave up and turned around. Tom, fearing they'd return with reinforcements, kept his Mario on and drove as fast as that big truck would go.

"Shoot, that was crazy."

"I know."

"How much more did they want?"

A little embarrassed, I said, "Five dollars."

"Five dollars? We almost got killed for five dollars?"

"It's the principle." Right, I should have just given them the money, and we could have skipped the racetrack. Live and learn.

Off in a field, we saw two large groups in fatigues, rifles on their shoulders, marching in rows in unison. Since they were marching in high kick and there was nothing indicating an army base nearby, Tom kept his foot forward on the gas pedal.

As we entered a small village, we passed two men dressed just like the high steppers, both on motorcycles, both with M16s (I guessed). The second we went by, they revved up and were on our tail.

What was going on? First, the Outlaws, now the Third Reich in hot pursuit.

"Should we stop?"

"No way," Tom said, eagle-eye focused.

"Are you sure?"

"Do you want to see your kids again?"

Good point.

A couple of miles later, Dale Earnhardt Jr. blew right through a military checkpoint, leaving Colonel Klink and Sergeant Schultz in the dust.

We continued the great race, but waiting for us down the road were eight battle-ready soldiers with I imagine a whole arsenal of bazookas, machine guns, and Winchester Magnums 45s in their boots, and hand grenades in their pockets. Probably a good idea to stop this time.

Though we weren't yet at a complete stop, Luis sprang out of the back. Immediately the uniformed men surrounded the truck, not afraid to make their weapons known. Love does not envy, but right then, I envied everyone in the world except Todd and Tom.

Luis, now our translator, told us, "He says get out of the truck."

Oh, my word, out of the truck. Do we floor it and get killed from behind, or do we face the firing squad?

No lip, just obedience. We were placed in a line.

The commander was dressed like Patton in pants that were tight to the knee then poofed at the thigh and a decorated wool coat. A swagger stick (the big, mean cousin of a riding crop) in one hand, he passed in front of us. His boots must have been too tight because he did not look happy at all.

He yelled something at Luis. Luis spoke back. Back and forth, they continued as I was kicking myself for dropping high school Spanish.

"Give him your passports."

Hold on there. That is not going to happen. If we turn over our passports, he will kill us, harvest our organs, and burn any sign that we ever existed. Not going to happen.

We all got out our passports. I whispered to the guys, "Don't let him have it."

The commander yelled something.

I said, "No," to whatever it was. *No* is one of twelve Spanish words I know. The eleven others are on a Taco Bell menu.

More yelling.

"No." I was either really brave or really stupid. It would not take long to find out.

Luis chimed in, "Lady, just give him the passports."

"No."

"But lady."

More yelling now, much closer to my face. Hmm, he had coffee con leche and bread for breakfast. Luis again, "Hey lady, lady, just do it."

"No."

Leaving the passport demand alone for a minute, Commander Yells-a-Lot started with questions. "Where are you coming from? Where are you going? Will anyone miss you?" The last one might have just been in my head.

After a short pause, he barked another order.

"He says you have to empty the truck."

Power hungry? Fine, I'd rather have him take my dirty clothes than the ID that gets me out of this country.

With everything spread out on the road, four of the eight went through every single bag, toolbox, and backpack. I neither envied nor felt terrible for the guy who opened the trash bag holding my dirty work clothes.

Luis pulled me aside. "You have to give him money."

"What? Why?"

"He won't let you go until you give him money."

"I can wear this guy down."

"But lady."

"Lady nothing," I sneered, a little tired of Luis, bribes, and "hey ladys."

Finally finished with the inspection, we were allowed to move it all back into the truck.

"Luis, tell him we are all set and we are leaving now."

"Hey lady, I can't tell him that."

All of a sudden you forgot Spanish? "Just tell him it is over and we are leaving."

"Hey, lady . . ."

"Luis, tell him now."

Luis translated. The commander came closer. I felt like the girl in Jurassic Park when Alan Grant said, "Stay perfectly still," while the T-Rex tried to figure out if she used strawberry or wild cherry blossom shampoo. I just looked straight in his eyes.

After I won the staring contest, he flicked his hand as if to say, "Go."

He didn't have to flick his hand twice. We got in and we went. Luis stayed behind. Maybe the commander was up for a game of dominoes.

Driving away, we felt like we had just been paroled after a twenty-year sentence. The joy that filled the cab could have filled a stadium.

Sometime later, Tom said, "If I could pay you ten thousand dollars to do that again, I would." He said the intensity he felt was ten times that of the first time he jumped out of a plane.

Good news for me. Now I don't have to try skydiving.

Envy messed us up, crossed our path, and nearly got us decapitated. The motorcycle drivers wanting more, the Commander expecting a bribe. I was envious too. I envied everyone, wanting to be anywhere other than where I was. But I love and love doesn't envy. I would not trade places with those I envied; then it would be them instead of me surviving potential kidnapping or worse. I love, and so I would not want anyone to have to go through that. Love that does not envy would rather go through pain than be envious of those who don't.

Love that doesn't envy is just happy for, admires, and is thankful for others' successes. It roots for, celebrates with, and congratulates.

Envy Disguised as a Good Story

Coming to terms with love that does not envy, I could see envy all over. When I willingly gave my opinion regarding what I deemed as someone's shortcomings by bringing up some juicy fact about someone or telling a story of pretend pity, what I was doing had nothing to do with love and everything to do with envy.

Some gossip is really envy in disguise. Often, that "secret" shared over a Biggby Macchiato spins a story to justify the retelling while ignoring the envy. "Did you hear that they are moving into a huge house? That is way too much room. Who would want to take care of all of that?" You, me, many people would love a beautiful big house. "Did you hear her son got into Harvard? I heard she wrote all of his papers for him in high school." I haven't personally asked Harvard, but my best guess is you don't get in if your momma writes your application essay. "She has never been on time a day in her life." Yes, because people like her and stop her to chat. "They are spending so much money on their vacation. Such a waste." A waste? No, vacations are memory builders without having to make the bed. I don't remember the couch we had in our living room when I was ten, but I sure remember that amazing trip we took to California. Positive that I was going to be discovered while walking down Mainstreet USA in Disneyland, I wore my Mickey ears just like Annette Funicello.

When we're envious of successes, talents, and popularity, tales told create wounds with words. A new car, helping kids with college tuition, a promotion at work are all fodder for gossip, masking monstrous envy. The Povichs wouldn't do that.

Envy of small things like long legs, thick hair, or high cheekbones could get in the way of fully loving my cousin Cheri, my friend Kimberly, or Sofia Loren (not that she'd know). Being envious of big things like fame, wealth, or power could stop me from appreciating the talents of others.

Love Without Envy

Envy is bondage. It ties you up and keeps you down. It creates a monster that steals happiness and robs contentment. Love that does not envy frees you to just love, not look or hope for flaws, but genuinely love and appreciate others. Love that does not envy removes the veil that only allows us to see the physical, such as appearances, wealth, and fame; it opens our eyes to the internal, heart, mind, and soul. Love that does not envy loves other people as they are, special, unique, and valuable. It is being content with what you have, family and friends being your true riches. "You're blessed when you're content with just who you are—no more, no less. That's the moment you find yourselves proud owners of everything that can't be bought" (Matt. 5:5 MSG).

Love that does not envy loves wholeheartedly without looking for flaws, hoping for falls, or uncovering faults. Real, pure, true, 1 Corinthians 13 love, loves everyone, no matter what they have or what they have done, or how many YouTube followers they have. Love that does not envy does not even give those things the time of day. Love that doesn't envy just loves.

Such a change in thinking. Something else to practice. How often has envy gotten in my way, ruined relationships, stopped the trajectory of my life?

The older you get, the uglier envy gets. To love without envy means you appreciate and admire without spite or malice.

Studies have shown that the more people use social media, the worse they feel about their own lives. Seeing social media friends' successes and seemingly idyllic lives brings people down. Way down. There is only one reason for that phenomenon: envy. Imagine a world without envy. Imagine seeing your Facebook family's posts and thinking, *Wow! Good for them* but never thinking, *Whoa, bad for me.*

I don't believe there is only so much good to go around. You go to a family reunion, and everyone wants a piece of Aunt Barb's special cake, but if you end up in the back of the line, you will probably miss out. Unlike dessert, there is no limit to goodness, successes, or moments to celebrate. With envy, if you see a friend in a fabulous marriage, your perspective of limited opportunity could tell you there is one fewer incredible marriage to go around and that you might get the short straw. But envy is deceptive.

Love that does not envy brings freedom. It shifts your behavior from keeping up with the Joneses to loving the Joneses and getting invited over for some of Aunt Barb's cake. No one wants to hang out with envy, vacation with envy, celebrate with envy. Everyone wants to be loved. Love does not go obsolete like cassette tapes and typewriters. Love isn't numbered like a Thomas Kinkade print or Hummel figurines. No limited edition, no special production, no going into the vault. Love is endless. Love that does not envy is genuine; its compliments are real, and its celebrating is legitimate. Love that doesn't envy is pure. It is bona fide, sanctified, justified. It is true love.

Lord, I have been so guilty of letting envy get in the way of fully, unconditionally loving. Please teach me to be content where I am and love everyone where they are.

CHAPTER 4

LOVE DOES NOT BOAST

Boasting. Another word that doesn't sound so good. In fact, it sounds really bad, and what does it have to do with love?

A Chinese proverb says, "Great boast, small roast." So funny and so true!

Boast, brag, show off, strut, flaunt, parade, pat yourself on the back—who does that? Better yet, who doesn't? Do you want to see pictures of my grandchildren? No problem! How about pictures of pictures my grandchildren drew? Got those too. If you have a minute to hear Cordelia playing the cello, watch a clip of Evayah's best drawings, or witness the comedic magic that is Rosemary on a trampoline, all I have to do is pull out my phone. I can keep you entertained for hours.

Being a grandma, I tend to travel in grandma circles. As soon as one grand reaches for her phone, hands dive into purses, pull out devices with screens the size of manila envelopes, and start pushing buttons to pull up media as quickly as possible so as not to be outdone by the other grand reproducers. With as many grandchildren as I have, my extra storage keeps a plethora of all that is amazing, wonderful, and captivating.

Love does not boast, but I sure do. How can it be wrong to want to show off your offspring's offspring, or your new car, or tell about the smart investment you made? Maybe the listener would want in on the action too. Really, it's a favor, a gift, sharing what they could have if only they were as wise, connected, or powerful.

But that isn't love, so says Paul.

In Haiti, limited funds have led to a lot of buildings lacking adequate rebar, quality concrete, and a good plumb line. Many of those crumbled in the thirty-five seconds the earth convulsed under Haiti in 2010, including a couple at Children of Jesus Orphanage.

One of my good friends, Lesly Tilus, runs the orphanage and school in Croix-des-Bouquet, just outside Port au Prince. After the earthquake, the first shelters for the children were large tarps that were soon torn and battered by winds and rains. A while later, large military tents were donated and became home for quite some time. Like the Haitian proverb "Little by little a bird builds her nest," little by little, Lesly began to rebuild. First, a dorm building split in two by a cement block wall held sleeping quarters for boys on one side and girls on the other. Then some plywood classrooms were nailed together. Every time it rained, the entire yard flooded, making it impossible for the children to have any space to play. So truckloads of dirt filled the place. I still have scars from shoveling and shoveling. I found out that I did not know enough Creole to instruct the drivers to inch forward as they emptied their load. That sure would have been handy. Instead, the kids played king of the mountain while I watched my blisters grow. After the dirt elevated the yard, concrete was poured, and the kids had a place to play again.

The hundred or so children ate their meals outside, and it was not unusual for white stuff to fly down from birds at the same time, sometimes right on top of the rice and beans. The kids needed a roof over their food, the next big project. So after a successful fundraiser, I brought down a few people from the United States, and Cristian, my Dominican son, brought a few more over the border to build an all-purpose room with a roof, no birds allowed.

Boasting Diminishes Others

At Lighthouse Projects in the Dominican Republic, Cristian's crew builds schools, water purification plants, houses, walls, and more. The buildings are sturdy and will withstand anything that Mother Nature throws at them, so says Cristian, but he's not bragging, not like his mom.

Cristian's crew for the roof-building project included Pastor Robar, a Haitian pastor who lives near Cristian just outside of Santo Domingo. Franklin and construction chief Felix were the other two who braved the border. Somehow the Dominican Republic let them out, and Haiti let them in—not an easy feat.

Our US crew of Tom and Todd speak English. Franklin and Felix speak Spanish. Pastor Robar speaks both Spanish and Creole, Cristian is fluent in Spanish and English, Lesly has mastered French and Creole, and I speak English and a little pig Latin.

After having supplies delivered, our crew began laying out a plan. Lesly was onsite and not thrilled about what he was seeing.

Just as we were about to pour our first footing, Lesly yelled, "Wait, that is too much rebar," in Creole translated into Spanish by Pastor Robar and then English by Cristian.

"Huh?" My English went quickly into Spanish then Creole. Apparently "huh?" is nearly the same in every language.

"You are using too much. We could build two buildings with the materials that you want to use for just one." Creole to Spanish, barely making it to English.

Cristian likes to say he was "born ready" and likes to think he was "born right." Knowing how it is done on the other part of the island, he had no problem telling Lesly that he was wrong.

Letting Lesly know that he is an expert at construction and knows what he is doing turned into lots of Spanish that got louder and louder as the Creole got faster and faster. Every few seconds I would interject, "What did he say? What are you saying? Wait, what?"

I got short answers. "He doesn't know what he's doing." "His buildings fall down." "He needs to just let us work."

Back and forth, Creole to Spanish, Spanish to Creole, words flying, tempers flaring, chests pumping. When a cockfight was about to break out, I jumped in the middle. "Stop! What is going on?"

"Lesly says that he does not want us to build the right way. I will not build a bad building. It is my way or no way."

Sometimes a translator needs to use a little discretion and not repeat everything verbatim. The sweet pastor was so caught up in the speed of the words, he didn't stop to think about the sting of the words.

"Just because that is how it is done in the Dominican Republic does not make it right," Lesly retorted.

Those were fighting words. Cristian turned red and smoke started coming out of his ears like Yosemite Sam getting mad at Bugs Bunny.

Pastor Robar translated Lesly's words. "I do know what I am doing. I have built many buildings. You are at my place in my country." Good point, Lesly.

"I don't care," Cristian said, smoke still spewing, "I'll go home before putting up crap. We work with plans and drawings put together by an engineer. We buy materials based on the list from the engineer, and we build the way the engineer expects."

Lesly, getting a little steamy himself, said, "I am an engineer," and we all went silent.

Oh, my word. Here we are, Dominicans and Americans, strutting our stuff, boasting about our accomplishments, bragging about our skills, and all along Lesly, kind, gentle Lesly, is an engineer, with a degree from a university. He really does know what he is talking about.

We were not showing Lesly much love.

Mark Twain once said, "Often a hen who has merely laid an egg cackles as if she laid an asteroid."

Cristian's cackling nearly kept us from building and kept the children eating under the birds. Perhaps we should have handled things differently.

If we had loved Lesly, the love he deserves from us, love that does not boast, the conversation could have been much shorter and a lot quieter.

It didn't seem like boasting, the bad kind of boasting, boasting that makes everyone else feel smaller. But it was. By boasting, the boaster is elevated above the boastee. My dad's stronger than your dad. My grades are better than your grades. I'm prettier than you are (it's a woman thing, never said out loud).

As soon as you are stronger, smarter, or prettier, the other person is weaker, dumber, and homelier. It puts you on a pedestal above the crowd, above the one. How can that be love?

The Bible mentions boasting a lot, and most of the mentions are awful. Jeremiah calls boasters fools and Ezekiel says that boasters are wicked and need to be taken down. Most of the boasting is about money, power, and status. Status! We all have the same status, right? We are all created in God's image, all created equal. Even Thomas Jefferson made sure to point that out in the declaring of the United States' independence, trying to do away with the belief that some of us are born regal while others are born ordinary. Nope, not one of us is better than the next. We are all regal, or we are all ordinary. I prefer to think regal.

The more I read what the Bible says, the uglier and more divisive boasting got. Of course, love doesn't boast. It became painfully obvious. Love recognizes everyone's shared value. Love doesn't compare and elevate. Love that doesn't boast is humble. Love that doesn't boast isn't better than, just different than. Different than makes for way better conversations, appreciations, and recognitions.

When the smoke settled, we began to work alongside the Haitians, learning from them as they learned from us. Appreciating them as they appreciated us.

Something much bigger than a building happened over the next few days. There is a prejudice between Dominicans and Haitians. In a country with few jobs, few classrooms, and few opportunities, Haitians cross the border seeking a better life. The poorest *barrios* (neighborhoods) in the Dominican Republic are Haitian. Haitians work like slaves in sugar and coffee plantations. Haitians are looked down on, as less than. Those hours of working side by side, learning some of each other's language, and mastering wordless communication broke down the walls of racism. Felix got to know Lesly's builder, know about his family, his favorite soccer team, and his dreams. Patrick became a person, an equal, who happened to be Haitian. Felix became a person too. We all did.

Boasting Divides

Boasting ignites tension; "different from" becomes "better than." Democrats and Republicans. Blacks and Whites. Dominicans and Haitians. But we are individuals, each with a name and a mom and a life, likes and dislikes, passions and beliefs. Our political leanings, neighborhoods, and skin color don't tell our individual stories.

My skin crawls when I hear someone call a whole people group stupid, ugly, or anything else that makes them less than. How often do you hear a Democrat call all Republicans morons? Or a Republican call all Democrats idiots? All, as in everyone. "They" dehumanizes. "They" are bad. "They" are stupid. "They" are evil. No, not they. There is no they. There is Danny, Jakel, Ann, and Natalia. No two are the same. Each with a name given to them by their mom and dad. Most other words are labels that we give people.

And it's not just politics. I grew up listening to my Catholic parents get into some rip-roaring arguments with my Baptist aunt and uncle, who felt obliged to save their souls because they were not "born again." My husband and I went to a Full Gospel church for years, and for years I defended and explained the Catholic faith to former Christian Reformed and Reformed Church of America friends. We all love the same God. We all have faith. We all believe that Jesus is the Messiah, the Son of God, is God, part of the Trinity, three in one. Yet we argue over issues of secondary importance and are often misunderstood, focusing on the differences rather than the common truth.

If God is for us, who can be against us? We can! The divisions among Christians are unsettling. Then politics sticks its gnarly head in the door and now you really have a standoff, Christians claiming that others can't be Christians if they don't vote a certain way. Because someone has a monopoly on all things true and right?

Families and friendships break up over the voting booth, church affiliations, and choice of spouse. Can't people have different opinions and still love each other? Isn't a relationship that lasts for decades way more important than who will be president for the next four years? There is such ignorance in thinking that skin color means anything more than heritage and history, that somehow the amount of melanin people have determines their intelligence, morals, or values. Different is just that. Not one better than the other. Allowing, recognizing, celebrating differences kicks boasting's behind.

People are people all over the world. I have talked to people who are afraid of Muslims. Muslims are individual people with their own set of beliefs. They are not all named Bin Laden. Just like Christians are individual people with their own set of beliefs. Not all of them start dispensing Kool-Aid.

When people stop assuming that all people of a particular occupation, country, or culture are just like the person doing something awful in a viral video, we can recognize that the person in the video is the exception, not the rule.

When we stop judging based on whatever standard we throw out there and get to know people by name, know about them personally, individually, so much changes. Imagine a world where we all take it one step further and actually love the person with different beliefs, customs, or heritage. Love the way we are told, directed, commanded to love. Love fulfills the law. Where there is love, there is no crime. Where there is love, there is no racism. Where there is love, there is no better than. We are all equal, all created in God's image, no one less or more.

I have a friend who says, "It's not good. It's not bad. It's just different." Can you imagine a world where love does not boast? A place that embraces the beauty of differences allows for open communication and conversation—a world where people can openly share without judgment and condemnation.

Besides the time when Jesus told us that we need to love each other, another favorite thing that Jesus said was to not judge. Talk about freedom! We are not the judge, not even the jury.

I love how Eugene Peterson translated Matthew 7:1–5 in *The Message*:

> "Don't pick on people, jump on their failures, criticize their faults—unless, of course, you want the same treatment. That critical spirit has a way of boomeranging. It's easy to see a smudge on your neighbor's face and be oblivious to the ugly sneer on your own. Do you have the nerve to say, 'Let me wash your face for you,' when your own face is distorted by contempt? It's this whole traveling road-show mentality all over again, playing a holier-than-thou part instead of just living your part. Wipe that ugly sneer off your own face, and you might be fit to offer a washcloth to your neighbor."

All we have to do is love. And love doesn't boast.

Lord, help me to see people the way you do, all equal with beautiful differences. And maybe not boast about my grandkids or my successes so much.

CHAPTER 5

LOVE IS NOT PROUD

LOVE IS NOT PROUD. REALLY? Maybe Paul got this one wrong.

Love is proud. I love and I am proud. I am proud of my kids, grand-kids, and euchre-playing abilities. I am proud of my friends' accom-plishments, my coworkers' successes, and my taste in clothes. I am proud of my coaching record, my players, and my driving skills. Lee Greenwood is proud to be an American. Merle Haggard is proud to be an Okie from Muskogee. James Brown is just loud and proud. Punch, peacocks, and Marines are proud. Everyone wants to make their momma proud. Proud Mary just keeps on burning.

Yet pride wins the first spot of the sinful seven. Pride is the death of some and swallowed by others. Pride keeps you from apologizing or asking for help. Pride got some angels evicted, is an abomination, and leads to destruction. It is the fuel that ignites a feud, ends marriages, divides families, and starts wars.

Arrogance and pride are fraternal twins; they stay pretty close together, often in the same verse, often one mistaken for the other.

Pride instigates all other sins, like boasting. Without boasting, pride would have no voice. Pride entangles and captivates hearts. All opposing ideas, perspectives, and beliefs are flagged by pride. Then boasting takes over with "I am smarter, more informed, and more enlightened than you." Arguments ensue, ears close as voices get louder.

Humility is the opposite of pride. It opens ears well before mouths. People listen to a humble heart, a humble delivery. Humble isn't loud or accusatory. Humble is gentle and humble listens.

My dear friend Jim Wilson exuded humility and was the unwitting poster boy for patient love. In my smarter, more informed, and more enlightened family, the longer you live the less you listen. By Jim's age, you know everything. Conversations included only the like-minded, reserving arguments for others. Jim was open-minded, always. He had beliefs, strong beliefs, opinions, and experience. Yet not a hint of pride impeded his heart, mind, or ears, as he thoughtfully listened and then spoke.

After years of working around the world with Youth for Christ, Jim started Careforce International, a Christian humanitarian, partnering organization working with people who had a passion, a mission, a vision to help people in need in their own country. Knowing the local people understood the language, culture, and real needs, Careforce would walk alongside helping with funding, supplies, a plan, whatever was needed, always working toward self-sustainability.

I came into contact with Careforce on my first trip to the Dominican Republic. Impressed by the unique approach, I called them the minute my feet hit US soil. Within a week, Jim and I were meeting face-to-face in his office in Burlington, Ontario. That day I joined the board, then had a chance to do some disaster relief work in a few countries and travel with Jim and Flo, his sweet, sweet wife. Traveling with Jim, I witnessed respect, kindness, and love for partners around the world. Never "Well, in Canada we . . ." but just sincere admiration and fascination, always learning, always growing. With scads of experience and truckloads of wisdom, Jim had plenty to share and freely gave it away, but only when asked and always gently. Never forcing an agenda or pushing his systems, Jim made you feel like his idea wasn't better, just another way of reaching the same goal. In reality, most of the time, Jim's ways were better. But you sure never knew that he knew that.

On December 16, 1999, torrential rains induced flash floods, destroying thousands of houses, leaving tens of thousands stranded in Vargas, Venezuela. Starting well after sunset in areas with sketchy electricity, no view of the storm gave warning. Young children were swept out of their beds. The relentless force snatched babies from their mothers' arms only to reach back and snatch the mothers too. Fathers clung to walls and families, not understanding the monster bent on dragging them out to a watery grave. Millions of gallons of water moved so much earth and debris, some areas were buried under ten feet of mud. Bridges collapsed, buildings crumbled, while cars and bodies were washed out to sea.

Tens of thousands were left homeless, and as many as thirty thousand people died. The waters separated families, with many hoping to find each other and terrified they wouldn't.

I flew into Caracas with my youngest son and a mission. My job was to see what was needed, figure out how to safely get it to where it was needed, and then make it happen.

Caracas is a bustling town with five-star hotels and one-star barrios. With a clear division between the haves and the have-nots, Noah and I were warned to stay far away from the have-nots and just hang where the haves do.

Our hotel opened its arms and our room invited us in. Marriott seldom disappoints.

After depositing our suitcases, we headed out into the capital to search for wherever we were supposed to go. God always seems to know the way. Luckily so did our cab driver. Through his little English and my bit of Spanish, we communicated pretty well. Andres agreed to be our driver for the next few days as we navigated our way through the congested city. First stop, a refugee center.

Love Does Not Compete

The Poliedro de Caracas seats twenty thousand people. The huge complex for concerts, shows, and sporting events was inaugurated in 1974 with George Foreman kicking some Ken Norton booty in just two rounds. It was too brief for fans, but George and his sons George, George, George, George, and George were still thrilled for the victory (or would've been, if they had all been alive at the time).

Just outside the arena's main entry were lists taped to windows and nailed to telephone poles. List after list, name after name; names of the missing, and names of the found. Each day new lists arrived from around the city. Mobs of children hoping to find a parent surrounded the rolls until huddles of anxious mommas pushed through, praying they'd spot their child's name. My chest tightens at the thought of that sight. How awful to be a child in a strange place, surrounded by strangers, scanning thousands of lines of ten-point type. How painful to be a mom, helplessly waiting for the next list to arrive. The lists were separated into the living and the dead. Lists from other refugee camps and lists from the morgue as bodies were unburied and identified. Weeping, wailing, laughter, explosions of joy, all melded into one somber song.

Working our way through the crowd, Noah and I no sooner stepped through the door when a yank on my arm nearly sent me to the ground. Attached to the yanking hand, a lovely woman with cheerless deep brown eyes.

"Americano?"

"Yes."

"Come."

Mary toured us all around, starting on the first floor and then headed up to more of the same. Mattresses carpeted every square inch of the cement floors, every closet, locker room, hallway, and even between rows of seating. Some mattresses were temporarily empty while others served a multitude of purposes: chairs, sofas, play areas, cribs, dining tables. Each held the belongings of the transitory user. Wall-to-wall mattresses with wall-to-wall people, some coughing, some sleeping, all living in shock.

Noah pulled out his digital camera and snapped a picture. The second he flipped the camera around to show a shot of three young boys sitting on a cot, the weighty fog muddling everyone's mood started dissipating, lifting the burdensome load. Like tween girls to a boy band, young children swarmed around him while he continued to click and show the marvels of modern picture taking. Before long, the hive began to shake with giggles. Contagious as measles, all around me smiles turned into belly laughs. The adults were enjoying the moment at least as much as the kids. Laughter really is good for the soul.

Overwhelmed and overworked, one lone man doctored the thousands. With people on top of people, sharing air, glasses, and toilets, viruses scattered like water from a sprinkler.

An extraordinary man, Dr. Gonzalez and his immediate family survived the storms, but a couple of relatives were among the missing. Severely understaffed with just two nurses rounding out the crew, the doctor did not have time to find anyone. I was honored that he found time for me.

"What do you need?"

"We have nothing but sickness. No antibiotics. No aspirin. No cough medicine. Not even a bandage."

"I will try." I have a Herculean aversion to making promises. Until I know that I know that I know, I really don't know and am the first to admit it.

Having learned the hard way that there is no use in sending anything if it is destined to be pillaged at the docks, I headed for the water. Mary came along for the ride. She spoke more English than the cab driver, and between the two, they were nearly fluent.

Men in fatigues were standing around a lot of buildings, same drill, different port.

"Who is in charge?" I asked through a rolled-down window.

"Ve allí."

Not understanding the words, I did understand the pointing finger. So ve allí we went.

Again through the window, "Who is in charge?"

Again some words and a finger.

Mary, Noah, and I ventured into an important-looking building at the end of a finger. There a man in a more impressive uniform sat behind a desk.

"I would like to see your boss."

A shrug and phone call later, the jefe of jefes welcomed us into his impressive office.

Explaining the needs of the refugee center, I then explained what I could do.

"I can get it here, but I need to know that it will all get to Peligro."

"Of course, of course."

He wasn't really convincing. "I can only get the doctor what he needs if I have a promise that the medicines will get to him."

"Of course, of course."

"How are your wife and children?" I said, testing the waters.

"Of course, of course."

Gracias and adios. I had to find a different way.

Back at the hotel, we bumped into a couple of men with a much larger nonprofit organization not far from mine. After hellos, I suggested that we work together to figure out the best way to help. While we were telling them where we had been and what we had learned, their eyes glazed over. Either I am a horrible storyteller or they were really tired. I know the context wasn't princess-and-dragon captivating, but I would have loved to have received the information I was giving them at the start of my trip. Skipping steps one and two, heading into step three, I would be a whole day ahead. They just shrugged me off. Hmm, pride? Love is not proud. I was not feeling the love.

Because God is so cool, there just happened to be a guy within earshot of the fruitless conversation.

"Are you here to help?"

"Yep."

"You have to meet my friend."

Sounded good to me. I never met this guy before and I was already feeling the love.

Walking out to the parking lot, I decided that if he drove an unmarked cargo van and offered me candy before getting in, it might be good to forgo the trip. Since we walked up to a beautiful BMW and there wasn't a sweet in sight, I felt perfectly comfortable getting into a stranger's car in a strange country with Noah in tow. Of course, of course.

Pulling up to what had to be the most luxurious hotel in South America, I decided if he offered me candy on the way home, I would still take the ride.

Waiting for us in the opulent lobby, Omar Vizquel was all smiles and happiness. We sat down on furniture that nearly swallowed me like an oyster. Rearranging a bit, I started to feel more like an adult and less like Edith Ann.

Omar, it turns out, is a professional baseball player, a shortstop from Venezuela playing in the major leagues in the United States. Omar contacted every Latin American Major League player, requesting their presence in Caracas for a softball game to raise money for flood victims. Everyone said yes, except one, who thought he was a little too big for this game. Pride. Later it was discovered that he had been dropping some pills, giving him power over the baseball, hitting it like no other, resulting in a fall off the pride pedestal.

We talked for a long time. Omar gave me his number so we could stay in touch.

No candy was offered on the way back. I would have taken it. I was really hungry.

The next day was more of the same. With Mary and Andres leading the way, the hours were filled with more refugee camps, more government offices, and more "of course" answers. Throughout the day, Andres and Mary told their stories as we searched for the right doors leading to the right person.

Andres beamed, talking about his wife and four children, all under the age of six, a man in love. High school sweethearts, at eighteen they wed with babies coming not long after. Driving a taxi gave Andres a decent income to support his crew.

Mary had not been able to locate her family in the month since the floods. Each day she scoured the new lists, holding her breath while reading the names of the deceased, audibly praying as she read the names of those found alive in other camps. Until the floods, Mary worked as a travel agent, a good job in a nice office with her own desk, phone, and stapler. When her building slid into the ocean, so did her job. She lost her family, home, income, and clothes, everything in one night, one long tragic night.

More doors, more dead ends, but Noah and I gained new friends who will stay in our hearts forever.

With the next morning not showing any more promise, my patience waned. We were far from home, all we wanted to do was help, and we ran into multiple roadblocks. By noon, I was vexed and hungry, genuinely hangry, which added to my resolve. Lord Jesus, something has got to give.

"That's it. Let's go to the palace."

"The palace?" Mary was confused. "For what?"

"We are going to see the president."

Giving a look that said, "This lady be crazy," Andres turned the car around and steered us in the right direction.

A sizable guy in uniform with a great big gun stopped us at the entry. His stern look wasn't overly inviting.

"Just tell him I am Kim Sorrelle, and I am here to see the president."

Words were exchanged. The military man stepped into the guard shack, made a phone call, then opened the gate.

A Door to the President

"When God closes a door, somewhere he opens a window," said Julie Andrews right before singing about her favorite things and figuring out that she could make clothes out of curtains.

Verbal instructions on where to park and what door to enter were given to the Spanish speakers. Andres started shaking a bit. I get it. Many guards, many guns, and probably many bullets can be a little intimidating. He opted to wait in the car with it running, ready for a quick getaway, thinking we would be just a minute.

Inside behind an old desk, another muscular fellow in a uniform a size too small and with pecs practically popping buttons questioned our presence.

Staring the uniformed man in the eye, with my jaw set and my pheromones exuding confidence, I said, "I am Kim Sorrelle, and I am here to see the president."

Bulging-biceps guy picked up the phone, said something, then hung up the phone and pointed to the stairs behind him.

At the top, we walked in on a news conference with lots of lights, cameras, and microphones focused on Hugo Chávez. A moment later, we were directed to sit down at a table in a big office.

No one said a word. We just sat in silence praying and waiting.

Several minutes later, three men entered the room and sat with us as we exchanged introductions.

"Hey, I'm Kim Sorrelle. This is my son, Noah, and my friend Mary."

"I am the minister of defense, and this is the president." Apparently, guy number three wasn't worthy of an introduction.

Hey, Hugo, how's tricks? I said in my head.

I spoke of Dr. Gonzalez, the conditions of the refugee center, and the needs. I told them that we had shipping containers full of medicines and medical supplies just waiting to hit the ocean. Then I looked Hugo in the eyes and said, "I am not willing to send the cargo down without your assurance that 100 percent of the contents would go to Dr. Gonzalez at Peligro."

Staring back, President Chávez said, "OK." Then he gave some instructions to the minister of defense. We stood, shook hands, and left.

Back at the hotel, two tickets to Omar's softball game were waiting for us at the front desk. Since we were leaving early in the morning after the next day, I didn't bother to exchange any more money before arriving at the stadium. We were invited into the dugouts, had seats close enough to tell who did and who did not shave that morning, and were caught off guard when we heard "Kim Sorrelle" come from the announcer's booth. Hugo shared the news of the coming medical supplies.

I was feeling kind of bad, thinking of people back home who knew every one of these players, where they play, their positions, hometowns, and batting averages. I didn't find out until later that Omar was kind of a superstar, a Golden Glove–winning shortstop. I was so clueless that I thought that meant he was also a boxer. I'm glad that I didn't say that out loud in a dugout.

Names like Pedro Martinez, Roberto Alomar, and Manny Ramirez filled the program. President Chávez took the pitcher's mound and pitched for both sides for a couple of innings.

More famished than my money would support, I bought Noah a bag of Doritos and a Coke. Since peanuts in the shell were almost half the price of Doritos and beer about a quarter of Coke's price, I used the rest of my bolivars. To this day, that is one of the best meals I have ever had in my life. It is amazing how great food tastes when you haven't had any for a long time.

Andres and Mary came early to take us to the airport. Hugging our friends goodbye, I split my US dollars between the two, gave Andres most of Noah's clothes and Mary all of mine. Noah and I boarded the plane with nearly empty hands but really full hearts.

Most people never heard of those terrible mudslides that took more lives than 9/11, Pearl Harbor, Jonestown, and Hurricanes Katrina and Maria combined. Days after the disaster, the world reached out; organizations and countries sent money and physical assistance. At first, President Chávez welcomed the aid. But it didn't take too long before he kicked everyone out and declared that Venezuela did not need any handouts, but they would take care of things on their own.

It was nearly ten years before there was some semblance of the way things were preflood. Thousands remained homeless, and Peligro and other refugee centers stayed full for many Christmases. Pride? If Hugo had loved people, he wouldn't have let his pride get in the way of rebuilding faster with help from others. Before that, he was thought of as a pretty benevolent guy who really cared about his people. He even allowed his wife to use part of the palace for displaced children right after the floods. By the time he died, not many were singing his praises. Love for people was not evident in his actions. Love is not proud. Love doesn't get in the way. Love accepts help because love knows that it can't always do everything alone. And love also knows that it is out of love that people want to help.

President Chávez's "OK" had heart. He showed love, put his pride aside, and cleared our containers immediately upon their arrival. Going one step further, he paid the cost of delivery from the port to Poliedro de Caracas. Not one bandage or bottle of cough medicine was pillaged from the contents.

About a year later, I got a phone call from that bigger organization that opted to work alone. Apparently, every container it sent was still sitting on the docks. They asked if I could contact my source to get their items distributed. For some reason, Hugo didn't take my call. He was probably busy helping the refugees. Pride, pride, pride.

The mission world is loaded with pride and humility. The humble ones are so easy to love. I have certainly been a member of the unlovable proud.

The days of missionaries standing on street corners thumping Bibles are over. Today, it is all about demonstration then proclamation. It makes so much sense. How do you tell people that Jesus is the bread of life when they have not eaten in a couple of days? Or talk about living waters that do not run dry when you are standing in Burkina Faso during a drought or watching children drink contaminated water that is sure to make them sick?

Matthew captured these words of Jesus, "I was hungry and you fed me, I was thirsty and you gave me a drink, I was homeless and you gave me a room, I was shivering and you gave me clothes, I was sick and you stopped to visit, I was in prison and you came to me" (25:35–36 MSG). Then Jesus was asked when those things happened, and his response was that whenever you do any of these things for people who are neglected, marginalized, overlooked, or ignored, it is like you are doing it for him.

Love that is not proud accepts help, letting other people love back. Humble love cares more about loving others and couldn't care less about what people might think. That garbage gets tossed in the ocean.

Such love does not care about looking weak, not knowing everything, or losing at table tennis. It listens with ears of love rather than formulating an answer before the talker finishes talking. Love that is not proud never sees the finish line, never believes that we have the market on all things right and true. Love that is not proud never stops learning or growing. And while it is at it, it opens others' hearts to you. Love that is not proud is humble, and humble is more attractive.

Lord, help me to recognize when I am prideful and not loving the way I should. Let me be humble like Jim Wilson and love like Mother Teresa. Please remind me to open my ears before I open my mouth.

CHAPTER 6

LOVE DOES NOT DISHONOR OTHERS

LOVE DOES NOT DISHONOR OTHERS. Dishonor does not honor, give credit to, appreciate the opinions of, or acknowledge the wisdom of others—the "others" we are supposed to love.

Dishonor is not just honor's ugly counterpart. We are speaking of pushing your beliefs, your grand wisdom, and your oodles of experience that certainly make you overqualified for the job of instructing everyone on what they should be doing, feeling, and believing. That's a mouthful, but real. Americans are the king, queen, judge, and jury of knowing not only how things should be done but also why, when, and where.

In *Codependent No More*, a book that changed my life, Melody Beattie introduces the concept of "unsolicited advice," so simple yet so revolutionary. Who wouldn't want advice? Great advice can save time, money, and marriages. If it weren't for people wanting advice, Dr. Phil, Dave Ramsey, and Oprah would be out of work. I ask for advice all the time. If someone knows something I don't or at least knows it better, I am not above getting a dose of free wisdom from the more experienced or more learned.

Unsolicited advice, however, is nails-on-the-chalkboard advice. It is hearing a friend's stories about the grade-school bully, snotty junior-high queen bee, or nightmare-inducing neighbor and being told you cannot possibly use the same name as that person, the one you had already chosen for your newborn. It is being crushed by your lucky-to-be-invited-wedding-dress-shopping future mother-in-law telling you that the wedding dress you just fell in love with makes you look wide. It's walking your parents through your dream house, the one that you just put under contract, and listening to them say you don't need that much space, the roof needs repairs, and the decorating is a little dated. It's the new girl in the office informing you the way everything was done at her old job. If things were so great, she probably should have stayed there.

Being told how to respond to a text from someone you met on Christian Mingle, to your boss when asked to take on an extra project, or to your children when they whine at bedtime without asking for any advice is demeaning; it is letting you know that you are not good enough at relationships, at your job, or as a parent. Unless requested, advice needs to stay in the mouth of the advisor.

Unsolicited advice is pull-your-hair-out, dig-your-heels-in, kick, scream, don't-tell-me-what-to-do advice. It is dishonoring. And it is relationship wrecking. Sometimes a friend just needs a listening ear. Agreeing that her husband is a jerk after she had an argument that put him on the couch the night before will totally backfire on you when they kiss and make up. Now you are the friend who thinks her husband is a jerk, maybe not a friend anymore.

Unsolicited advice, the kind that is dishonoring, can come in different forms. There is the obvious "if I were you" and "this is what you have to do." Some advice is less obvious, not so blatant, not so in your face. Advice meant for you but spoken to someone else can be equally, if not more, damaging—in fact, so not in your face that it is done behind your back. Behind-your-back dishonoring can be equally, if not more, damaging as well. Stories tend to be told differently when the main character is not present. A friend shares the great news that her son just earned an engineering degree. Congratulations ensue. Sharing the news with a mutual friend is great until adding, "Well, she practically did his homework for him when he was in middle school." That is dishonoring.

Speaking broadly, a few people have questioned my work in Haiti over the years in a couple of ways. First, by stating that there is so much need at home and I should be helping in my own country before helping abroad. Second, claiming that nothing good will ever happen for the impoverished nation because some Haitians practice voodoo. Both so dishonoring. Yes, people need help everywhere. The homeless in my city, families facing food insecurity, and people going through a crisis all need help. The questioning, however, discredits the work and degrades the choice of where to help, dishonoring the person. Where's the love? Defaming all Haitians and excusing their mistreatment, lack of opportunity, and extreme poverty based on what? Hearsay? Movie scenes with voodoo dolls and animal sacrifices? Not genuinely understanding but making harsh judgments shames, damages, and dishonors, elevating the one doing the talking.

The United States State Department estimated in 2018 that more than 85 percent of Haitians are Christians while 2.1 percent practice voodoo as a religion. Praying the Lord's Prayer and asking for daily bread takes on a whole new sincerity in a country where half of the population live on less than a dollar a day while 80 percent live on less than two dollars a day. With the average cost of a loaf of bread at $1.66, praying for the Lord's provision comes from deep within, requiring faith on a whole different level.

Dishonoring, Not Knowing

Lack of knowledge can lead to a lack of compassion and an abundance of dishonoring—a lack of love. Misunderstanding, not really knowing someone, and questioning motives can also lead to dishonoring. I will never forget, nor let my mother-in-law forget, the time I was asked to bring the birthday cake for a small family party for my boyfriend, later my husband. It was just a few months after we started dating and I had only met Steve's parents a couple of times. My seventeen-year-old inner baker was shaking in her boots. I decided to bake a chocolate cake from scratch.

As we pulled up to his parents' house, I was so nervous that the cake would not live up to Steve's mother's standards. As soon as we parked, Steve's youngest sisters came running out to the car. "Mom said it's probably a crummy box cake," eight-year-old Jennifer shared.

Oh, my word! A crummy box cake! We made box cakes for every birthday growing up. The mix, some water, a bit of oil, and a couple of eggs, everything needed to make birthdays, anniversaries, even the elementary school carnival cakewalk special. I salivate thinking of the Duncan Hines strawberry supreme cake with canned cherry frosting that made it from the mixing bowl to the dinner table every September for my birthday. Are they really crummy?

This woman must make everything from scratch. She probably bakes her own bread, cans homemade pasta sauce, and wouldn't even think of buying a packaged cookie. The thought made my head spin. I grew up eating Wonder Bread, Chef Boyardee spaghetti, and Hamburger Helper. The only thing homemade at our house was my dad's oatmeal, and even then it was Quaker's quick oats. *What happens when I marry this guy and buy noodles in a box?*

I was so relieved that I had made a cake using cocoa, flour, and sugar instead of a premade powder from Betty Crocker. Imagining trying to live up to the culinary standards Steve was used to put a pit the size of a cantaloupe in my stomach. Those words, "crummy box cake," advised me that I had better start working on baking, roasting, and sautéing skills if I was going to be the wife that Steve deserved. I did not ask for that advice. At that moment I felt so less than, so inadequate, so small, so dishonored.

Later, the pit was removed when I discovered that Steve's mom was no Julia Child after all. She used French's packets to make everything. Sloppy joes, gravy, meatloaf, you name it, there is a French's packet for it. At Christmastime she would buy banana bread from the store, wrap it in foil, and gift it to the neighbors as her own. The only homemade thing coming out of her kitchen was green bean casserole, if that can be considered homemade. My in-laws and I laugh about it from time to time. Steve's mom has never believed that I made his cake from scratch that day, but I did, I promise.

In Haiti, we Americans give all kinds of unsolicited advice. We assume (and you know what that means) that our methods are unequaled, our teachings unparalleled, and our knowledge unsurpassed. It can be easy to think that way when you see infrastructure and technology that go back to the 1940s. It's not about introducing Hoover's "chicken in every pot and car in every garage" ideology, but clean water and food every day would be nice. We have a handle on those simple things. We must be smarter or, at the very least, know more, so our advice will be not just warranted but welcomed. In reality, the American way is not the only way and often not the right way in other cultures.

Dishonoring and Judging

While I was waiting for a connecting flight in Fort Lauderdale, my eye caught a woman who looked absolutely bewildered. Everyone at the gate would soon be flying to Port au Prince. Men in fatigues, businesspeople in suits, groups with matching T-shirts, Haitians going home or to visit family, all were people with a mission.

One of these things was not like the others. That lady did not belong.

Standing alone with a steamer in one hand and wedding dress in the other, she did not look like a UN police officer or a businesswoman. Bob Sieger was jamming on her T-shirt and between her paper-white skin and blond hair, I hypothesized that she likely wasn't Haitian.

"Hey, are you OK?"

Tears began to well up in her eyes. Karin had met a man in college and was flying to Haiti to get married.

Haiti is not a typical destination wedding kind of place. There are a few resorts on the ocean, but I have never seen an ad enticing couples to let their "dreams come true on the white sand beaches of the Haitian coast." Passing Chilean UN Minustah personnel perched behind machine guns on the back of Humvees doesn't really shout "Let's get married here."

"He is stuck! The travel agency stole his money!"

That's horrible. Poor thing, so happy to be marrying Mr. Right, but Travel Agent Wrong messed things up.

With her fiancé's plans in turmoil, Karin's plan was to arrive in Port au Prince, hail a cab, retreat to the nearest Holiday Inn Express, and wait for him to straighten out the mess.

There might be one or two little roadblocks on the way to consummating that plan in the Land of Mountains.

First, a taxi. There are plenty. You might end up where you were hoping to go. You might even get there with your luggage. It's possible that you will also depart with your purse. If you do not negotiate a price before making the trip, you will definitely be way overcharged. You will definitely see your life pass before your eyes at least three times during Mr. Toad's wild ride. And, once seated in the cab, you will for sure regret it.

Second, a hotel. There are some. No Holiday Inn Express. But there is the Habitation Hotel, Le Plaza, Visa Lodge, and a couple of others not far from the airport. The hotels may or may not have rooms available, and finding out could be pretty tough if you don't speak French or Creole. You also need to know that you can't run your toothbrush under the faucet or something else will be running within a couple of hours. Toilet paper goes into the basket next to the toilet, never flushed, no matter the content. Electricity will not necessarily be available twenty-four hours a day. Air-conditioning is not standard, and a woman the color of mayonnaise ferrying a puffy white dress and steamer might just be a target for some funny business. But maybe not.

Karin followed me over to my group, the only group not wearing identical shirts.

"Karin is going to be staying with us." Taking my unsolicited advice, skipping the cab, likely saved her life or at least her suitcase.

Some baffled looks followed by the slightest head bob were all I needed to know that my team was totally on board.

During the two-hour plane ride, Karin revealed more of her story. A divorcée from Spokane, Washington, she left three teenagers home alone to marry a guy she met at the local junior college. It had been love at first partner project. Her fiancé was not with her because his visa expired, and he had to leave the United States. Though from Nigeria, Isa Snake had flown to Ecuador only to have a travel agent snooker all of the money that Karin sent to him via Western Union. All three times. Not once. Not twice. Three times.

"You might want to get a new travel agent." Unsolicited, but obvious.

The story went on. Karin left her husband, the father of her teens, for Isa.

Out of 195 countries in the world, Americans can enter 159 without a visa. Nigerians, just 26. With the field narrowed, Haiti was chosen for the nuptials and three-week honeymoon.

Only three years older than her firstborn, who had just passed his driving test, Isa, of royal blood, owned a recording company and import-export business. Extremely intelligent, exceedingly hand-some, and entirely charming, poor Prince Snake was a victim of a corrupt government in his native land. The royals were kept from their funds for ridiculous political reasons. His enormous inheritance had to be transferred to a US account for him to gain access. For some cockamamie reason, the US banks were withholding the cash, a simple error really, which would quickly get rectified when they returned to Washington as husband and wife. Logically, Karin was fronting the funds.

"So, where were you supposed to be staying?"

Again with the tears. "An all-inclusive on the ocean."

I didn't bother to ask the name of the all-inclusive since I do not know of any Haitian resort with multiple restaurants, a beautiful gazebo hanging over the Caribbean serving as the perfect backdrop for vow reciting, plush robes and slippers waiting in the closet, rose petals in a heart shape on the bed, an exotic spa with couples massages, or even a ping-pong table. And I could not think of one oceanside resort where I would want to spend three weeks.

Now, of all times, this is when love does not dishonor others. How do I honor that? How do I not share my many years of experience building wisdom? I would be saving her, helping her see the light. Isn't that what we are supposed to do? Lead people to the light? My light is on high beams and hers has run out of batteries. Love does not dishonor others. I was trying not to think that my way was the better way—that my path out of her unrecognized predicament beat the heck out of her path of thorns leading to a cliff. *It's serendipitous; we were meant to meet. She doesn't know it yet, but time will show her how desperately she needs me. I will make the sacrifice. I can be her Captain America, just a tad shorter and a little higher BMI.*

After landing and maneuvering customs and immigration (what would she have done with that mess?), we gathered our suitcases, walked through the throngs of pushy cab drivers and grabby porters, making it safely to Patrick with our chariot awaiting.

Chariot might be generous. Tap taps are small pickup trucks with a metal roof over wooden benches in the back. In Michigan, a tap tap would seat eight; in Haiti, twenty-one.

The twelve of us, one security guard, eleven backpacks, thirteen suitcases, one wedding dress, and a steamer filled the space like twenty-one clowns in a Volkswagen Beetle. Stifling heat, honking horns, barking dogs, polluted air, and traffic jams welcomed us to Haiti.

Our Holiday Inn had no air-conditioning, no television, and most of the time, no electricity. But being greeted by forty smiling faces beat private rooms, miniature bottles of shampoo, and a one-cup coffee maker any day.

While hugging and high fiving our welcoming committee, I felt tugging. A bride-to-be was stretching out my shirt. Karin was anxious to email her beloved. Shocked to find out there was no electricity, thus no internet, Karin got teary again. Afraid that she was going to dehydrate, I brought her up to the concierge level, floor two of the orphanage, where thirty guests share two bathrooms and five bedrooms.

Probably not the newlywed suite she envisioned for what should have been her wedding night.

I reminded myself, I will not dishonor her by questioning her decision to leave her husband for a nineteen-year-old community college student no matter where he's from. Maybe her husband was a louse, and the nineteen-year-old is really amazing. Or maybe she traveled 3,418 miles to find out that she'd been hustled. But I loved her, because I was supposed to, so I would not dishonor her. Plus, right now was a horrible time to enlighten her. Had the travel agent not been a thief, she would have been Mrs. Snake by then. Instead, she had to share a room with strangers, after being introduced to this loud, dusty, hot country that looks nothing like the brochures for Sandals Jamaica.

Usually the first to rise, I was surprised the next morning to see Karin in the dining area so focused on a computer screen that she startled when she heard me fumble for a coffee mug. The power was on. That's always encouraging.

Before I could even get out the *good* in "good morning," she said, "I have to go to Western Union right now."

Great, she wants to send the Snake more money.

Poof, the power company pulled the plug. That was the first time I was thankful for no electricity, ever. Although it could have waited a few minutes to keep the water pump running, because I was hoping for a shower.

Relieved to have had a minute to put the right words together and inform her that she has been scammed, I then remembered that love does not dishonor. She knew the guy, I didn't. Maybe I was just cynical. Right.

When everyone was up, ready to go, Karin went to bed.

Returning from spending the day with the residents of Sisters of Charity Home for the Sick and Dying, the greeting party of forty-one smiled wide, but no one wider than Karin.

"I have to go to Western Union now."

Welcome home.

Love was not my facial expression. Hot, tired, and worn from hours of rubbing feet, applying nail polish, and braiding hair, three words that I did not want to hear were "Western Union now." Those ranked right up there with "no dinner tonight" and "your account's overdrawn."

"It's closed." Probably, maybe, hopefully, true. Love, kind love, patient love.

My team, with their buckets of wisdom, decided to give me some solicited advice. I needed advice. I had invited her to join us, so it was up to me to figure out the best way to help. They agreed that I needed to lead Karin to the truth. Easy for them to say. I was the one who had to do the leading. So, after meeting with my team, I met with Karin.

"I found a ticket; I have to get him the money right away."

"You could buy the ticket from here, save the Western Union fee, and he could just go to the airport and hop on the plane." Unsolicited advice, but so wise. Shake the bushes a little, see if he's really planning on coming.

I couldn't convince her.

Another night on the computer, another demand for a ride; again we left too early and returned too late. I dropped a few hints that there was something fishy going on. Trying hard not to dishonor her, I told her a heartbreaking story about "this one woman" who fell in love with a much younger Haitian guy, married him, and then found out he just wanted a green card.

"That's horrible!"

"I know. So sad. It happens all the time, young guys taking advantage of older women."

"Yeah, that's dumb. I can't believe that woman didn't see it."

Kettle? Are you listening?

"Have you ever known anyone like that?" I asked. Maybe the woman in the mirror?

"Nope."

Karin did not understand that I was saving her. She would thank me later. But I planned to hold back the "I told you so."

Again, in the morning, "I have to go to Western Union."

Again, "It's not open yet."

Again, "I have to go to Western Union."

Again, "It's closed."

Four mornings in a row. Four evenings in a row. Karin's frustration was growing as my understanding of dishonoring love was shrinking. Praying for answers, I kept asking, "Lord, what am I supposed to do? It's none of my business, but here she is. It seems so obvious, but maybe what I think is wrong."

Then day five.

"I have to go to the airport."

"It's not open yet. Wait. What?"

"I bought a ticket like you said."

"Is Isa almost here?"

"I'm flying to Ecuador."

Because of what I said, however I said it, Karin would be taking off in a couple of hours and arriving in Quito thirty-six hours later. Because she bought a ticket.

Chicago is about the same number of miles from Fort Lauderdale as Port au Prince is from Quito. By plane, Chicago to Fort Lauderdale takes roughly two and a half hours. You can drive from Chicago to Fort Lauderdale in less than twenty hours. Imagine my befuddlement at a thirty-six-hour flight. Was Isa messing with her?

"Thirty-six hours?"

"Yes, I fly to Fort Lauderdale, then to New York, I'm there overnight. Then I fly to Miami, then to Ecuador."

I did suggest she buy a ticket.

We asked her to stay in touch and post some wedding pictures.

A few days later, when the power was on, there they were, posted on her Facebook page. Karin was beaming. The prince looked pretty happy too. She looked great in the big white dress that she carried from Spokane to Fort Lauderdale to Port au Prince to Fort Lauderdale to New York to Miami to Quito. She was wise to bring that steamer.

About a month and a half later, I heard from Karin again. She sent me a text asking Will's marital status. Will is the strongest and best-looking fireman in Haiti.

"Will is still single as far as I know. Why are you asking?"

"You are not going to believe this, but Isa is a fake!"

"Oh?" Who saw that coming?

While they shared such happiness during the ceremony, their reasons for happiness were not shared. Karin, so happy to marry her Prince Charming. Isa, so happy to secure United States residency. He did not marry for love; he married for a green card. Instead of a romantic wedding night with champagne, chocolate-covered strawberries, and whispers of undying love, Karin slept alone as Isa wandered into another woman's boudoir. Karin realized that she had been scammed.

Lord, what should I have done? I thought I knew what honoring love meant so I bit my tongue, sort of, then she bought a ticket. I didn't know what to think. But now I believe I understand.

I thought that I was better, higher, smarter, on a different level than Karin. I was not showing love that does not dishonor others. Thinking I am better made her less, and that's what I got wrong; that's where love was left out. I might have more experience in booking airline tickets. I have seen marriages start with deception and end with heartache. I have been taken advantage of a time or two, feeling sorry for someone and sending money only to find out later that the funds bought Air Jordans instead of paying the rent. But more experience does not mean better. More of anything, schooling, money, possessions, does not equate to being higher on the human ladder. We are all on the same rung.

Speaking frankly to Karin could have saved her some heartache and a lot of money. She might still have made the thirty-six-hour trek to South America, but maybe not. Helping her, in the right way, rather than avoidance in apparently too subtle of hints, would have really been love. Love for her, love for the person sharing my ladder, meant letting her know what she could not see. Her love was blind. I was wearing glasses. Not speaking with her had nothing to do with avoiding dishonor.

Honoring Others with Shared Experience

Sharing experience, knowledge, insight, is not advice, solicited or otherwise. Love shares what it knows to be true to help those you love to avoid disaster, increase success, or deepen relationships. Sharing without advising is the trick. Advice is an opinion typically in the form of a recommendation to guide someone's actions. An admonition, a warning, caution, guidance, urging even, with an expectation that the advisee will take heed and change the trajectory of planned actions. Love that does not dishonor shares with no expectations, knowing that the ones you love do what they choose, not what you choose for them.

I learned that it is all right to give advice when asked, so long as you don't ignore the "when asked" part. Even then, I realized that advice is an opinion. I looked up sayings on opinions and found a lot of them, all really saying the same thing. Basically, opinions are like pennies, plentiful but not worth much, best thrown into a wishing well and then left underwater forever. Sharing your opinion should open the door to listening to the other person's opinion. When you think that your opinion is the right one, the only one, you are not loving in an honoring way. Be open to listening, a patient-love kind of listening, and allow people to have a different opinion without believing that your opinion makes you better, higher, above. Love that does not dishonor others does not say that all the people in that political party are idiots. By criticizing anyone who casts a certain vote, attends a different church or no church at all, dresses differently, lives differently, has different color hair, tattoos, or piercings, you are dishonoring them. Putting them down means putting yourself up.

Love that does not dishonor does not look at the outside but wants to know about the inside.

I have seen families break up because they voted differently. Voted. On paper that seems so silly. How many Thanksgivings have ended poorly because politics or religion became a topic of conversation? Inevitably both parties walk away steaming, sure that they are right, smarter, and the other is wrong, dumber. Conversations are not confrontations. Two completely different things. Insisting, pushing your belief, opinion, or wisdom on someone is not conversation. Blood pressures rise, hormones go nuts, and before you know it, there is no turning back. Honoring love would have a conversation, listen, acknowledge that the person you are talking to can think differently from you, but that does not make them less. How often do we go from calling someone by name to calling them a name? How often do we dishonor?

Lord, please help me to listen, allow, realize that we are not all the same, but we are all equal. Give me discernment to know when I am sharing information or advising with expectations. Let me know when to speak and when to just listen. Remind me often that I am not above anyone for any reason. That we are all created in your image and you love all of us, just as we are to love everyone, without any notion of superiority but always with equality. Help me to love with a love that does not dishonor others.

CHAPTER 7

LOVE IS NOT SELF-SEEKING

THERE IS A DIFFERENCE BETWEEN self-seeking and selfish. You can pick out selfish in a crowd. The guy at the office who drains the coffee and doesn't make more. The woman who walks right past the line into the next available bathroom stall. The kid who never gives his friend a turn playing Minecraft. That's just plain selfish.

The one story that I remember from grade school catechism was about a boy who always snatched the biggest piece of cake, scrambled to get the best swing at recess, and squirreled away the best toys. Never sharing anything or caring about anyone. His parents decided to teach him a lesson. One day the boy's mom made her award-winning cream puffs, a dreamy dessert with a delectable puff pastry filled with luscious Chantilly cream generously topped with a decadent chocolate ganache. A true work of art, a heavenly creation. (Catechism was way after breakfast and just before lunch, which is why I remember the description of the mouth-watering masterpiece nearly verbatim.) She purposely made one larger than the others and whipped fermented salmon heads, haggis, and tripe into the rich cream (I'm a little vague on those details). When the platter of pastries was passed, it was no surprise that the boy took the biggest one. Anticipating a tasty delight, he took a big bite. His eyes opened wide and began to fill with tears as his taste buds met the gross concoction. While all the others enjoyed their dessert, he ran from the table into the bathroom where who knows what happened. Man, did he learn his lesson. After that day, neither the boy nor I took the biggest piece of anything ever. That boy was selfish.

Self-seeking, however, is much, much stronger. It is hotly pursuing, hunting down, sniffing out what you want, for your benefit, for your own happiness, furthering your interests, and advancing your goals, often at a cost to others. While selfishness is annoyingly obvious, self-seeking can be pretty sneaky.

A couple of years after the earthquake in Haiti, an American director of a small charity sent out a cry for money to save herself and the children who lived in her orphanage. She reported that shootings were happening all over Port au Prince. Gangs were going from house to house pillaging, ransacking, injuring, even killing innocent people. As the sounds of the gang's shouts and gunfire grew closer, she knew that the children were in imminent danger, and she had to flee. Unable to wait for the safety of daylight, courageously she gathered those precious souls and escaped the orphanage. In the blackness of the night with only the moon to light their path, the small tribe made the long trek to the US embassy. They huddled together in the dark, waiting for both the staff to arrive and donations to appear. Contributions would pay for a new place, a safe haven for these beautiful, parentless children far from the chaos of Port au Prince. This woman was brave beyond measure, self-sacrificing, putting her own life on the line for these little angels' lives.

Nearly instantaneously, money started pouring, no, gushing into the charity's US mailbox and bank account. Generous hearts were so touched by the story that they couldn't write checks or push the PayPal buttons quickly enough. Some probably searched their sofas for loose change and gave up their lunch money, anything to rescue those children.

My inbox became inundated with cries for me to leave the country, find cover, seek refuge away from the horribly dangerous city. Although I was staying not far from what was described on the charity's website and Facebook page as the epicenter of this ongoing criminal activity, I hadn't heard any reports of gangs with guns terrorizing the city. Asking around, I couldn't find anyone else who heard gunshots, knew of killings, or felt like they were in anything but the usual danger that comes with living in a big city in a poor country.

A few days after the alarming reports, a friend of mine happened upon the charity director in the area of Port au Prince that she had reported as a war zone. My friend told her we had not heard of what was published on the internet and wanted to know more about these gangs of thugs. The charity leader scoffed and told my friend that she just doesn't know how to raise money.

That is self-seeking, a total disregard for anyone else, pursuing an avenue to further her own interests, solely concerned with her own desires. The creation of such fear and trepidation led a team of surgeons to cancel their trip to Haiti scheduled for the following week. My heart still hurts for all of those who would have been helped. The surgeons weren't the only ones to change their travel plans. All because of self-seeking.

That is not love. Because love is not self-seeking.

Love that is not self-seeking considers everyone before themselves. Easier said than done.

Sacrificial Love

During my time of focus on non-self-seeking love I had a long flight, long enough that even the lowly coach riders were served a meal. I sat in the back row with just one other person sitting across the aisle from me. I was so hungry. I hadn't eaten since breakfast and the flight took off at four in the afternoon. I was running late, so I didn't have time to grab anything in the airport and looked forward to the who-cares-what-when-you-are-starving airline food. It seemed like it took hours for the flight attendant to serve everyone in front of us.

By the time she neared the back row, passengers looked around, hoping the growling animal was caged. But the growling animal was not caged. The growling animal was my stomach.

The pretty woman in the navy-blue skirt and blazer with the lovely red scarf tied around her neck finally made it to the back. Holding a better-late-than-never tray, she looked at both of us.

"Sorry," she said as she smiled, "but there is only one meal left."

My eyes welled up and my heart began to race. *Lord, do I really have to love this interloping vagabond who probably ate a big, juicy cheeseburger just before we got on the plane and likely has a backpack full of snacks when I haven't eaten for hours and only have three Altoids and a piece of wintergreen gum?*

Love is not self-seeking. I am supposed to love this guy, snacks and all. Sigh.

"He can have it," I said in my head, but it must have also been said with my mouth, because through my watery eyes I saw the one tray of food, my only hope for sustenance with hours of flight ahead of me, pass before my very eyes and onto my row mate's tray table.

I loved the traveling voyager.

I learned that non-self-seeking love hurts sometimes. It is not always easy. Learning to think of others, all others, first, before yourself, is a challenge. It might be easy to give your child the last meal, a bit tougher to relinquish it to a stranger.

Finding love that is not self-seeking to be this painful on an airplane traveling to Palm Springs, I feared the torture that awaited in Haiti.

When Others Seek Their Own Desires First

People joke about *Haitian time*. Typically, that means twenty minutes to three hours later than the digital time illuminated on a cell phone. In Haiti, "I will pick you up at three," is typically followed by, "Is that American time or Haitian time?" "Ha, ha, ha!"

On this trip to Haiti, I discovered a new definition.

Day two was much like day one. Even though sleep had provided a new outlook, new energy, and new patience, the newness started wearing off when my ride was a no-show at 8:30 a.m. By 9 a.m. Haitian time was getting on my nerves, and as 10 a.m. approached, everything new was old again. Finding alternative transportation, not always easy in a place far from a tap-tap route, I made it to the warehouse at 11:34 a.m., just in time to buy lunch for a staff member, his wife, and a couple of hired hands.

The warehouse was bustling with people moving boxes while others waited by trucks, everyone excited to receive items sent to them from America, items that are exceedingly difficult or impossible to buy in Haiti. No internet, no power, no shade from the hot sun, but great to see old friends' smiling faces. (Friends who live daily with no internet, no power, and no shade from the hot sun.)

My to-do list was long and not getting any shorter. Moving boxes was not on my agenda for today but weaseled its way in.

Finally, at 5:35 p.m., with darkness coming and a conference beginning with a 7 p.m. meeting, we locked the gate.

I had reservations at a guesthouse, Haiti's version of bed and breakfast, near the conference site. Haiti has few street signs and even fewer numbers on buildings. Finding the guesthouse was the first challenge. Challenge number two was realizing that booking.com was not precisely accurate when "quiet neighborhood setting within walking distance of the Conference Center" meant "a bustling commercial area three miles downhill from the Conference Center." Opting to stay at the much more expensive conference center hotel and hearing the front desk manager say "sold out" slapped down challenge number three. In baseball, I'm out.

While driving to find accommodations, the conversation in the car shifted, and so did my plans. Patrick mentioned translating for groups in areas outside of Port au Prince. Since he works full time for Rays of Hope, I probed a bit.

"When do you do this?"

"When they need me."

"So, like a day or two?"

"Naw, week or so."

"And you have to stay in some other area of the country?"

"Yep."

Hmm. Patrick works and gets paid a full-time salaried wage, a good one. A really good one. And lack of work to be done is never an issue.

"How long have you been doing this?"

"Like a year." A year? Physically drained and unfed, I feared love might be hanging on, but patience was losing its grip.

"Just one or two weeks?" One or two weeks, no big deal. I could live with that and talk it through with Patrick. Explain why this isn't exactly kosher.

"No."

I had to ask. "Three?"

"No."

My voice began rising in sync with my blood pressure. "How many weeks?"

"I dunno. Maybe twelve, fifteen." Twelve or fifteen, what? I tried some deep breathing while guns were backfiring in my head. Understanding that it starts with me, in my mind I questioned his training. Did I clearly explain my expectations? Did I plainly go over his job description? Did I specifically tell him what it meant to be a salaried employee? Yes, yes, and yes! Plus, I had said to him that if he ever had a chance to make some extra money to let me know and we would see if it could work out. But a third of a year? What was he thinking? What were *they* thinking?

"Patrick, you were working for them when you were supposed to be working for me all those weeks?"

"Yea, but it's not like they paid me or nothin'." They didn't even pay you! You translated for them, out of town, a week at a time, and they didn't pay you! Of course, they didn't pay you because I was paying you.

Grinding, well beyond gritting, my teeth, I said, "Patrick, this is not how this works. If I pay you, that means you work for me."

"But they needed me." Patrick, bless his naive heart, lives to be needed. Patrick is a do-anything-for-anyone kind of guy. He is a pleaser and works hard to make everyone happy. If Patrick can find a way to make something work, he will do it. He loves everybody and everyone loves him. His personality is infectious, his smile triggers joy, and his heart is as big as his country. For Patrick to work for others while getting paid by me elevated my frustration to a level beyond conception. But it was understandable from Patrick's point of view. He knows that our work together is never-ending. Doing a job that had an end and getting right back into his regular work made perfect sense. Not to me. Not to any American. It certainly shouldn't to these gentlemen whom I introduced to Patrick and who knew full well his employment situation.

Staring forward, seething, not so much at Patrick as at these men of the cloth who jeopardized Patrick's employment, I said, "I need your phone. I have to call Peter." Peter, the guy stealing from my organization, was about to get Patrick fired.

"He's drivin', you might not get 'im."

"How do you know he is driving?"

"Cause I was just with 'em up north but had to come back to get you."

Had to come back to get me? *Had* to leave the guy who isn't giving you a dime to pick up the signer of your paychecks? I *had* Patrick call him and tell him that I *had* to see him as soon as possible. Peter *had* no idea what I *had* in mind for him. To make sure it remained "in mind" and "in hands," I told Patrick to hide the tire iron.

At 7 p.m., instead of enjoying a nice glass of Merlot while getting to my meeting buddies, I was sitting on a roof in Sarthe meeting with a few of the people who had worked very hard at chiseling away at my patience. Love. Love that doesn't envy, boast, or is proud had me onboard. Patient, kind, not easily angered took a dive.

"Nice to see you guys." Not a lie, I needed this settled. I jumped right in. "You know Patrick works for us full time, right?"

A collective, "Yeah."

"So, you realize we pay him to work full time."

Again, "Yeah."

"I just found out that twelve or more weeks of this last year, he was doing work for you and not for us."

"So?"

Why was this so clear to me and so unclear to these men? Is it a man thing like when the green status light would be on and my husband would shout to me from the kitchen, "Are the dishes in the dishwasher clean or dirty?"

"So, you had him working for you knowing that we were paying him?" Seriously? This sounded a lot like self-seeking and nothing like love.

"Sure, we know that, but what he does in his spare time is none of your business."

Wow, spare time? None of my business? If Patrick needs a loan because of a *spare time* family emergency, it becomes my business. When we helped him get enough money to move from a tent to a house in his *spare time*, it was my business. When he or a family member has needed a doctor, hospital care, and medicine that were obtained during his *spare time* with extra money from me and others, it sure seemed like my business. But apparently spending twelve weeks translating for their organization while being paid for those same twelve weeks by my organization, during his *spare time*, was none of my business. *Breathe, love, just do it.*

"We pay him to work full time, fifty-two weeks, all year."

"Kim, you have got to read this book."

What? How did we go from "you are robbing my ministry" to "let's go read a book"? What book? *The Miracle of Mindfulness* by Thich Nhat Hanh to calm my last nerve that they were currently squashing? *The Art of Happiness* by The Dalai Lama XIV to somehow make me happy to be bamboozled? The Bible? I don't recall reading, "Exploit your neighbor as you exploit their staff." What book could possibly justify this unscrupulous behavior while teaching Patrick that it is A-OK?

"It's all about outcome-based performance. Who cares if Patrick is working five hours a week or fifty?" The pastor went on to tell me that sometimes he works ten hours a week, and sometimes he has to take a phone call as late as nine at night. So long as he is getting his job done, the number of hours does not matter. This, coming from a director of programs at an international mission. Did he solve all injustices, feed, clothe, house, and bring medical care to the entire world population while I had been unloading containers? It seemed like Fox, CNN, and MSNBC would want to get ahold of that story.

I repent of it now, but in that moment I told myself that it would be hard for me to take business advice from this man. He may be a wonderful pastor. He has a degree in theology. He is probably pretty smart. He has traveled the world. I am sure he is a great husband and father. He loves the same Jesus that I do. He reads. In fact, he has read *a* book on business—a book, as in one book. I devour business books like a lion devours a zebra, and right then, my inner lion wanted to pounce on his inner zebra.

"Pastor, there are some jobs like that," I said ever so patiently if that is possible with daggers flying out of my eyes. "If a job requires producing five hundred widgets daily, it really doesn't matter if it takes five hours or eight hours, as soon as the five hundredth widget is made, you are free to clock out. Then there are other jobs, like mine. I have never gone to bed at night thinking all of my work is complete. There is always more to do. Patrick's well-paid job is the same."

"Just read the book, Kim, then we will talk when we get back to the States."

I took a deep breath and tried to unfurrow my brow. "Tell you what." (Patience, love is patient and kind.) "I will just take Patrick off salary and pay him when he works for me, and you pay him when he works for you."

"Oh, Kim, Kim, Kim. I can tell that you're angry. Let's not make any decisions right now. Wait until we are back in the States, and you are well rested, then we can talk on the phone."

Let's? I didn't realize this was a collaborative decision. I didn't ask advice or seek his pastoral wisdom. Well rested? Just because I looked like I had been moving heavy boxes in the hot sun all day (because I had been) did not mean that I was not well rested. I was running on pure Haitian coffee and adrenaline, wide awake, thank you very much.

"I am not angry." (Hangry maybe, since I had not eaten since breakfast!) "It's fine."

"Man, Kim, you sound just like my wife when we are arguing, and she says *fine*."

That kind of did it for me. As close as I was to the edge, Peter's words sent me over without a parachute. I am not your wife. I am not *fine*. I am living a year of love (working on "love is not self-seeking," having already become a yellow belt in patient and kind love), and you are blocking me. How am I supposed to love you when you steal my employee, think that it is perfectly *fine* to use his *spare time*, jeopardize his full-time employment by taking him off the job for not one or two but *twelve* weeks last year, and patronize me on top of that! Love?

Gaining some control over the raging fury within, I said, "I shouldn't have come. This is between Patrick and me."

Smug, shaking his head, he said, "Kim, Kim, Kim." Does he see triple? "You need to just take it easy," he said as if I were Cujo and he was trying to talk the rabies out of me. I'll take it easy, all right. I'll take it easy in some bed in some yet unknown location as far away from here as possible.

I stood, placed both palms flat on the patio table, leaned in, and said, "You are the biggest, most chauvinistic, arrogant, self-seeking #$@&%* in the world!"

That's what I wanted to say, but love. So instead, I just stood up and said, "Goodnight, gentlemen."

"Kim, don't forget to call me when you are feeling better." *Lord, really? I have to love this guy? Can I strongly dislike and love at the same time? Could you maybe take a minute and rethink "everyone"? Are some people just downright unlovable? Because if some are, this guy is their emperor.*

After observing Peter's style of leadership, commitment to his choices, and dishonoring attitude, he undoubtedly topped the class in Self-Seeking 101.

But I loved this guy, or at least I did a few hours earlier. Now I had to bring that back again, reel it in. I didn't like his behavior in this situation. I completely disagreed with his reasoning. But I chose to love him. Right then, showing love was a *bit* trying, a *bit* as in it might take me a *bit* to drive from New York to Los Angeles. Love him.

I have discovered that deep breathing helps a *bit*. Maybe there is more to "cleansing breath" than I previously realized. There is something about sucking in air, no matter how polluted, filling my lungs down to my toes, that calms my soul and refreshes my brain.

In through the nose, out through the mouth. Again. Again. No exhaling fire, that's good.

The shower sure felt good that night. It happened later than I expected since my luggage left with my driver and did not return until the morning's wee hours, but good all the same.

Trusting God with Our Needs

I discovered that love that is not self-seeking looks out for everyone, puts everyone's needs and desires before its own. Not looking out for number one, trusting God will do that, allows us to do what God wants us to do. If we are not self-seeking, we are everyone-else-seeking. Seek goodness and blessings for others. Seek peace, comfort, and joy for others. Look for ways to help them be successful. Think of the things that you currently seek, and seek the same for everyone else.

Now, love that is not self-seeking does not mean ignoring your own needs. If you are not good at taking care of the things you have, it can force you to put yourself first. If you don't get your oil changed and your car goes kerplunk, you might have to use the money you have been saving for a family vacation. If you don't take care of yourself physically, not only will medical bills eat up that Disney trip, but you may have to self-seek and have others take care of you.

No matter where, no matter with whom, at work, home, book club, the PTA, love that is not self-seeking leads like Jesus. A servant-leader. Look for ways to help others find joy, grow, and prosper. Often it's surprising how quickly people follow your example and jump on board.

Contagious Love

When I think of all of the leaders of organizations I know, a few understood love that is not self-seeking way before I did. Shelley tops the list. A decade or so ago, she moved her family away from the comforts of American life with twenty-four-hour electricity and a Biggby on every corner for a much different life in Haiti. Shelley learned that most of the kids in orphanages have a mom or a dad, but in a country with an average annual income of just $450, it is impossible to feed, house, and clothe a family on $1.23 a day. So she rented a house and taught mommas how to make jewelry so they could bring their children home, giving birth to Apparent Project. Now that living-room jewelry store is a multi-building facility with potters, seamstresses, bookbinders, papermakers, and jewelry makers, all making a living wage. The scope of her influence is gigantic. Community development, prenatal care, medical relief, the list of finding what others are seeking goes on and on. Always giving a hand up, out of poverty, the number of lives changed is uncountable. Shelley knows that love is not self-seeking.

Love that is not self-seeking grows! It's contagious. It's fun. Not seeking everything for yourself but seeking everything for everyone else is such a happy way to live.

I did not realize how much self-seeking I was doing. By caring more about what Patrick was doing to my organization, my, my, I was not seeking what was best for him. He is talented, kind, and admired. Living love that is not self-seeking, he is always giving away his last gourde and the shirt off his back. Having the freedom to work for whomever, whenever, opens new doors of opportunity that will help many more than if he is working for only one organization.

I learned that non-self-seeking love hurts sometimes; it is not always easy. Learning to think of others—all others—first, before yourself, is a challenge. When you realize that looking for goodness for others is love at its very core, love becomes much more of an action than a feeling or an emotion. Love that is not self-seeking has feet; it walks the walk. Love that is not self-seeking authentically congratulates, absolutely wishes well, actually celebrates. Love that is not self-seeking gives the last meal, a place in line, an open door, the last seat, room in the lane, and the biggest cream puff.

Lord Jesus, I know that I have been a self-seeker in so many ways, seeking success, pleasure, and, more unfortunately, sometimes at a cost to others. Help me to live love that is not self-seeking. Open my eyes to seeking justice for others because I love them, all of them.

CHAPTER 8

LOVE DOES NOT EASILY ANGER

Love does not easily anger. That sounds right but, man, I can get my anger on.

The whole world became a blur as the sun rose just for us that day. I floated down the church aisle on clouds of happiness to the loon's perfect harmony while woodland creatures fought over window seats, and herons and egrets craned their necks, hoping for a glimpse. Steve and I locked eyes as we locked hearts, tossing the keys into the great abyss. "I do." Two perfect words on such a perfect day. No two people were ever before or forever after so in love.

But when the honeymoon was over, Steve peddled my dreams for a ticket to nightmare city. He didn't know how to put the top on the toothpaste, his socks in the laundry, or his dishes in the sink. Muddy shoes dirtying the carpet, things tossed willy-nilly, and the toilet—hadn't he been practicing his aim for years? But the thing that sent my blood pressure into stroke range was his deliberate disregard of my selflessness, cooking, cleaning, laundry. Absolutely no recognition.

Mercury in my anger meter rose at the rate of his unconscious neglect. Cinderella got hitched to the wrong prince.

I decided to give him one more chance. Leaving work early, I prepared his favorite meal, lasagna and German chocolate cake. Wedding gift candles and placemats prettied the table while Barry Manilow prettied the mood. When all of the food went in the oven, my curling iron, mascara, and slinky little something came out. Certainly, the magic I created would yank him out of the Land of Oblivion.

I spritzed a little Calvin Klein Obsession just before he opened the door.

Wearing a sultry grin, I let my satin robe expose a shoulder.

He said, "Hi," and kissed my cheek as he brushed by me to change out of his work clothes. Great start.

Not really noticing me or the candles, he sat down and dug in.

After giving him ample time to say something, I said, "Do you like it?" Why should I have to ask?

"Yeah, it's good."

Good? That's what three hours in the kitchen gets me.

By the end of dinner, anger took over and served cake. I was mad that he didn't say anything about how I looked, how dinner tasted, or that time he forgot to pick me up, and then some residual forgetting Valentine's Day got thrown into the fire.

"You haven't said anything!" Right into a fever pitch.

"What do you want me to say?"

"How about 'great dinner, Kim' or 'you look beautiful' or 'this is so sweet of you,' anything!"

"Why are you mad at me?"

Isn't it obvious?

I yelled something, he yelled something, I yelled while he yelled, and we both yelled some more. When I finally relinquished the floor, he said something I will never forget.

"It's not my fault. It's your expectations that got you mad."

I threw my fork into the sink, the same sink he apparently didn't know existed, and stomped out of the room, shouting, "You can sleep on the couch tonight!"

I was hot. First, Steve doesn't say anything he is supposed to, then he slaps me with "your expectations." This is *my* fault. He's blaming *me* for this. What the flip. My expectations! Really? My expectations. Hmm, really, my expectations. Doggonit, he was right. In the moment that made me madder, but after that day, my attitude shifted from "he is such a jerk" back to "dang, he is so good-looking."

Anger, I can do anger.

Patience Instead of Anger

Working on finding out more of what love means, I had my doesn't-easily-anger love put to the test.

I already had the drive to Burlington, Ontario, the headquarters of Careforce International, down to a science. Filling up with gas before hitting the road, I could go the entire five hours without my gas tank or my bladder emptying.

In Canada, Lay's makes ketchup potato chips, Tim Horton's owns real estate on every corner, loonies and toonies jingle in pockets, gravy and cheese curds smother McDonald's French fries, marijuana is legal, and throwing away prescription medicine is a crime.

Careforce received a take-all-or-none donation of medical supplies that were desperately needed in Ouagadougou, Burkina Faso, West Africa. In the "all," some expired boxes of pills were part of the booty. Since the United States doesn't care what goes in the trash, I stuffed the boxes into the back of my crossover and headed home. Working late put me at the border around midnight with a 3 a.m. bedtime.

Crossing the border was always the same, same patrol guys, same questions, same answers. I pulled up a bit ahead of schedule, eager to feel a pillow under my head.

"Where are you coming from?"

"I was visiting friends in Burlington." Not a lie, not the whole truth, but the minute you say you work there, the border goes from five minutes to an hour.

"What do your friends do?"

"Mostly charity work."

"Where are you going?"

"Grand Rapids."

"Why?"

"I live there."

"Do you have anything to claim?"

"Nope."

I started to put my car in gear, expecting the usual, "OK, you can go."

Instead, I heard, "Pop the trunk."

Oh, shoot. I forgot about the boxes. Clearly, he wouldn't think that I should have declared the forty boxes of whatever medicine from the all-or-nothing donation. I wasn't too worried in my head, but I forgot to tell that to my body. My heart overreacted; sweat came from out of nowhere, landing on my forehead, and my left eye started twitching. An audible "Great, he's going to think I'm winking at him" was followed by a throat clearing outside my window.

"What's in the trunk?"

"Just some expired medicine from a donation that we got, that my friends got, my charity friends got. And in Canada, you can smoke weed, but don't you dare throw away old pills. See, we had to, they had to take everything or not get any of it, so they did and this was . . ." Love does not easily anger. I will not be angry at the donor. I will love them and their generous donation.

My rambling hurt my chances of a quick exit.

"I need you to pull up right there and get out of the vehicle."

It's a car. Why don't they ever just say "car"?

"I can explain." Like Lucy "splaining" it to Ricky.

He snorted, took my keys and cell phone. "Save it."

Save it for what? What is it that I was supposed to be saving? Remember, love does not easily anger. I love this guy. I love everybody.

"Just give me a second to . . ."

"Get inside."

Get inside? I never have to get inside. Inside is for drug dealers, smugglers, and serial killers. Inside is seedy, probably gray, and really dirty. Not for people like me, innocent, pure of thought, truthful, and kind. I love. Shoot, I'm practically Gandhi.

I turned to ask his name and saw that he was beaming, practically glowing, giddy even.

Ah, now I get it, I'm getting Punk'd by the TV show that plays elaborate practical jokes on the most unsuspecting people. Why didn't I wear the blue dress? It is so much more flattering and goes better with my eyes. I probably have bags under my eyes. I should say I have to go to the ladies' room and do a quick makeover. Do cameras really add ten pounds? Ten pounds in my blue dress might be all right but not in this tweed outfit. Who wears tweed anyway? What was I thinking? This is a national television show and I'm wearing tweed. Great.

"Sit."

"Can you show me to the ladies' room first?"

"No."

No? First "sit," then "no." I'm not a cocker spaniel. It's part of the gag, right? Fine, I'll sit. Nice, one empty bolted-down chair, the middle of the three. It probably still holds DNA from the Boston Strangler. I wonder if the guys next to me are in on the gag. They must be. Great costuming, right out of Hoodlums R Us. I wanted to joke with them and say, "Hey, what are you guys in for?" but I was ordered to save it. I am not angry.

Twenty minutes went by with no cameras, no Ashton Kutcher, and no acting surprised. As I started to panic, just a little, realizing this might not be part of a television show, I became desperate for it, couldn't wait any longer for it, pleaded in my mind for it, even in tweed.

Several men in uniform huddled in the middle of the noncriminal side of the room. Their murmuring was incomprehensible. I was sure that any second they would yell, "Break!" and fling their arms in the air like a basketball team. Nope. Eventually, they just unhuddled.

My guy, whose name I still didn't know, grabbed a cart and headed outside. A few minutes later, he was back with the boxes. Then all of them were giddy. Either their shifts were almost over, or someone was moving and really needed boxes.

My guy was getting pats on the back, high fives, and *way to go*'s. Cell phones emerged and posing started. Everyone took a turn with the boxes, one foot on the cart, the other on the ground, arms crossed, guns flexed, trying not to smile. I began to wonder if these guys might be a little touched. They were brown cardboard boxes for goodness' sake, not Cindy Crawford or Naomi Campbell. (What I wouldn't give for those cheekbones.)

The pictures got uploaded and sent to Texas, where all the action happens. I heard things like, "This is the biggest one ever, it's gotta be." Biggest what? I still hadn't been told anything. As far as I knew, I could be getting busted for baby aspirin. Love does not easily anger.

"Let's go."

I followed my guy into a little room where the lone female in uniform was waiting.

I didn't get strip-searched, but a little getting to know each other first would have been nice. Gum wrappers, receipts, tissue, paper clips, something sticky, and a couple of loonies were dumped out of my purse as I was taken back to Ted Bundy's chair.

My chair mates changed while I was on my date. This time I did say, "So, what are you in for?"

Twenty-something-year-old green hat guy spoke first. "Seeds."

"What were they? Poppy seeds?" So funny at two in the morning.

"Pot." Whew, way worse than baby aspirin.

I turned my attention to scruffy-beard guy with whom I was sharing half of Norman Bate's chair.

"Papers."

"Papers?"

"Yeah."

Seeds. Papers. Not the greatest conversationalists. Fortunately for them, I can hold up both ends of a conversation like scruffy-beard guy could probably hold up both ends of a boxcar.

"You?"

"Baby aspirin."

I told green-hat guy that his mom was not going to be happy and he'd likely be staring at cowboy wallpaper for a long time.

A patrol uniform materialized, tossed keys to the seed boy. "Don't do that again."

Since I was picking my jaw up off the floor, I missed the exit of the boy who would be grounded. I've been here for hours for nothing and pot boy gets a slap on the wrist and sent on his way? Who's making these rules? Love, love, love.

I had had just about enough. I stood as tall as any five-foot-one-and-three-quarter-inch person could. "What am I doing here?"

They laughed. Isn't that always the way. When you are not even trying to be funny, that's when they think you are. My guy gave a queen's wave that I took as a summons to follow him. In some other little room, a mustached man behind a desk looked up. "You are in some big trouble, little lady."

Little lady? Where are we, the O.K. Corral?

"For what?"

It turns out that it wasn't baby aspirin but prescription Benadryl. Evidently, in a town just south of mine, they make a lot of meth using Benadryl. I thought you got to that euphoric feeling all by yourself; now they have a drug to get you there. An illegal drug it turns out. And the "biggest ever" was a drug bust that put El Paso to shame.

I tried to get out the explanation the first patrol guy told me to "save," but mustache guy wanted me to "keep it" for a while longer.

Since the cat was out of the bag, the uniforms started talking about this infamous day that finally put little Port Huron on the map. I guess when you are bringing in guys for seeds and papers, a pallet full of dope is liking winning the Mega Millions lottery.

"I didn't know."

"Ha!"

What is it with men and one-syllable words and noises?

"Seriously, I just want to throw it away."

I got funnier all the time. This must be what Jerry Seinfeld feels like when he is doing a stand-up routine.

The more I said, the louder the laughter. Pretty soon, hands cradled bent-over bellies and slapped bent-over backs.

They practically made a tunnel for my guy's departure; it was a 4 a.m. kickoff.

His icy stare caught mine. "You are going to jail for a long time. It's Friday night, you can't even get bailed out until Monday morning." Love, not anger.

I was drained, my bladder was bursting, and I had a good book. Jail sounded pretty good, like going on a spa weekend without the spa.

Scruffy-beard guy and I got pretty tight. Three beautiful children, an attractive wife, and a Labrador retriever were waiting for him. Somehow, he forgot his birth certificate, which gave him an extended stay at the Bates Motel. His bride had to wait until morning to overnight it. His cargo was expected on Saturday afternoon. So the expecter got the weekend off.

I did find out a couple of other things from the man with extra facial hair. Not only was Benadryl a coveted drug-making ingredient but my "crime" was "way too big for Homeland Security." I'd have to wait for the big guns to arrive from Detroit.

He was right; I don't think this was his first rodeo.

At 6:18 a.m., John Wayne sauntered in. Again with the queen's wave, I sauntered behind him.

What's with the queen's wave? It was like Disneyland's mandatory two-finger point. I wonder how much practice it took to make that wave so understandable.

My purse and briefcase beat us into the mustached guy's office.

Barney played with the lone bullet in his chest pocket, saying, "We got us a big one, Andy."

"Now Barney, don't be jumpin' to conclusions."

"Better call Aunt Bee, tell her we're gonna be late for cobbler."

I hallucinate a little if I don't get my sleep.

I finally didn't have to save it anymore. Andy let me tell my story. I explained the whole thing, that we got a crappy donation, couldn't throw it away in the land of maple syrup, Uncle Sam doesn't care, it's a Christian humanitarian organization, and I'm a missionary, not a drug producer. Do you really think I'd be wearing tweed if I was hauling down that kind of scratch? Maybe not my exact words.

"My only crime is I'm naive."

"I believe you." Thank you, Lord Jesus, Andy sees the light.

"But we are going to have to keep the boxes."

Perfect, no sense in overloading my dumpster.

Smug, spent, and arms full of belongings, I walked out of that office a good three inches taller.

"Give the lady her keys, boys."

The celebrating warriors turned mangy hyenas froze. My guy had the keys. No one seemed to know where my guy put the keys. My guy left hours ago. My guy didn't just leave but was driving north for the weekend—north, maybe with my keys, for the weekend. *Now I'm angry, but it took a while, even though it wasn't easy.*

After a phone call revealed a denial of possession, a search began. I have had valet parking before. They always have a board with little hooks where the keys hang waiting for vehicle owners to return. Is it really so much trouble for Alcatraz to have a little board with hooks?

I sat back down on Jack the Ripper's chair, between scruffy-beard guy and a new guy who had suspicious bottled water, or some other stupid reason. Like me! Stupid. This is stupid. Yes, I am mad.

Twenty-three minutes and thirty-seven seconds later, "Got 'em." I wanted to grab that young man in blue, kiss his face, and give him both of my loonies and my firstborn.

I could not drive away from there fast enough. The second I hit the road, I started bawling, tears flowing from my dehydrated eyes. All of the pent-up emotion, keeping it together for so many hours, I just let loose. I was scared, intimidated, and angry, mostly angry. Then relieved when my previously sleeping son answered on the fifth ring.

"You won't believe what just happened to me!"

"Who is this?"

Well, that was sobering. "Your mother, who could be in jail right now, who just got busted for crossing the border with a record number of drugs, who was just freed from Stalag 13."

"Mom, did you take some of those drugs?"

With sun and moon both AWOL, antagonizing rain, fog as thick as motor oil, a sudden thump, thump . . . thump, thump began. "I have a dang flat! You gotta be kidding me!"

"Mom," he said, using the same tone you'd use to talk someone off a ledge, "pull over."

Parking my good-for-nothing, empty-trunk car in front of bushes that housed carnivorous predators, I flung open the good-for-nothing door and defiantly stepped out into the sinister inkiness. I punched my fists in the air, turned my face to the sky. "Lord Jesus! Are you on sabbatical?"

Drenched and way more than miffed, I tramped around that rapscallion piece of dung, that stupid pile of all things unholy, kicking each tire. I started with the two on the driver's side. Great, the bad one was on the really dark side, near Cujo and the velociraptors. I karate kicked the back one so hard if it wasn't flat already I was sure my powerful roundhouse would bring it down. But no, so, the front right it is. I approached it with such disgust, thinking of all the ways that I was going to torture it before feeding that lousy hunk of rubber to the ravenous crocodiles.

Giving it the same death kick, I was surprised when it did fight back. It was solid, whole, unblemished. I looked toward the heavens again. "Sorry, my bad."

Taking off slowly, everything felt pretty good. I went a good half a mile before the thump, thump . . . thump, thump returned. That is when I realized I was driving over the reflectors in the middle of the road.

Slow Anger and Communication

Love does not easily anger but I kind of did. Sitting in that chair all night gave me a lot of time to think. In the Old Testament, there are several instances of God being angry. Mostly over injustice in the form of slavery, racism, and abuse. But what sent him over the edge was when people who knew better were the ones doling out injustice. There is an expectation that when you know what is wrong, you don't do it, a valid expectation that does not require mind reading. God took a long time to get angry because he loves. He could have smitten me so much sooner, perhaps using the "wait until your father gets home" tactic. The angry wrath will walk in the door at dinner time, give you a good talking to, and send you to bed hungry. But love.

Love that doesn't easily anger communicates. Long before the throwing of the fork, I should have told Steve what was bothering me. Sure, it took me a while to boil, but I could have kept the teapot off the flame entirely.

Fast anger typically reacts poorly, forgetting love. Slow anger that builds with no one but you and your hairstylist knowing, puts love in the corner. Love that is slow to anger, the right kind of love, doesn't erupt suddenly or build to a crescendo. Not-easy-to-anger love talks, listens, watches, slows the heartbeat, breathes before reacting, gets the whole story, and sees the whole story. Not-easy-to-anger love puts love above anger, so it doesn't forget about love. The kind of love that is easy with grandchildren, but much tougher with your own, especially after a long day.

Mr. Cleaver practiced love that did not anger easily. He would calmly sit on Beaver's bed and have a talk with the boys. Wally and Beaver learned a lot more during those talks than they would have learned from Ward's belt. He was definitely a slow to boil kind of guy.

Love has to stay in the driver's seat with anger riding the bumper. If anger tries sneaking in through the back window, love needs to just put the pedal to the metal. Anger might be along for the ride, but love should not make it comfortable.

Love first. Love calmly. Love love.

Lord, I have gotten angry so many times without loving. Forgive me. Help me to breathe, stay calm, and love, really love.

CHAPTER 9

LOVE DOES NOT KEEP RECORD OF WRONGS

I HAVE BEEN DREADING "LOVE does not keep record of wrongs" most of all. I have put it off, charging ahead with "easier" words like protects, trusts, and hopes. I didn't want to do this one because I knew I would not be able to go down the "remember the time when you . . ." path again. I would have to stop telling stories of when I was wronged, reminding people of when they wronged me, or sitting in a little self-pity pool full of wrongs against me. I would have to burn the record book, erase my memory, and not participate in the "he said what?!" conversations. Mostly, I have been avoiding this one because I would not be able to tell this story again.

A group of pastors from Missouri who had never traveled to Haiti asked if I would be their guide. They were interested in a water project that I had been spearheading.

According to the World Health Organization, 3.4 million people die every year due to water-borne illnesses, making contaminated water the number one killer. Cholera, just one of many diseases, has affected more than 800,000 Haitians since it was introduced into a main water source in 2010, killing nearly 10,000 people so far. According to the World Bank, only 24 percent of Haitians in rural areas have access to clean water. So 76 percent drink contaminated water. Adults miss work, children miss school, babies die. Many people get their drinking water from the same rivers used for bathtubs, washing machines, latrines, waste dumps, livestock watering holes, and swimming pools. So when the pastors asked if I would help, I couldn't say yes quickly enough.

Eight Missourians, two Haitian friends, and I arrived in Arcahaie, an area north of the capital, before noon. Even with some of the nicest resorts resting on its coastline and roots of the most glorious mango trees running deep, clean water, electricity, jobs, and education are as scarce for the 130,000 residents as most everywhere else in the country.

The local church affiliate arranged for our lodging. Our Hilton for the next five days was a small two-room building surrounded by a concrete block wall with chunks of broken glass cemented into its top. ADT Haiti. Each room had four twin-sized beds and not much space for anything else.

After taking a tour of the property, the chief pastor pulled me aside.

"Hey, um, did you see the rooms?"

Since that was about all there was to see, my answer was pretty obvious. But before I spoke, I went through the whole scenario in my head . . . He is asking me because there are ten men and me, a woman, again obvious. He thinks that I wouldn't be comfortable having men in my room, a place that is only used for sleeping since the heat keeps you outside until you are ready to call it a night. So since I have no problem sharing a room, I would say, "It's OK, I'll sleep outside."

Then he would say, "No, if anyone should sleep inside, it should be you."

To which I would reply, "I'm happy to share a room."

Then he would say, "Oh, that's great, there are only so many beds." And I would smile and all would be well.

"It's OK, I'll sleep outside."

This was when my head scenario took a sharp left turn.

"Oh, that's such a relief."

What?

"There are men here that would be uncomfortable with a woman in their room."

Really? Do they sleep naked? Are they afraid that I will attack them in the middle of the night? What would I possibly do in a 10-by-10-foot space between the hours of 10 p.m. and 6 a.m. in a 110-degree room that would make others uncomfortable? I don't snore, sing, or talk in my sleep. I wear a T-shirt and shorts and they stay on just fine all night. I'm a fairly skilled sleeper; I have been practicing pretty much every night for my whole life. I lie down, close my eyes, and before I know it the sun is up and so am I.

I stood contemplating what just happened. I know that women have burnt their bras, want equal pay, and can now be on the front lines in battle, but this kind of liberation is a little extreme. I am all for men opening doors, giving up a seat on a bus, and sending flowers, especially sending flowers. When the check arrives, I offer to pay but am perfectly happy letting a man pick up the tab as his momma instructed, and who am I to come between a man and his momma.

As the men were choosing their beds, I was working on finding mine. I looked at the truck. I could sleep in the back of it, but what if it rained? I could sleep in the cab, but the heat would be unbearable. Then I saw an interesting apparatus. To call it a table would be generous. A piece of plywood was held up by two Haitian-style sawhorses. We brought along an air mattress that would fit underneath, on the hard, rocky ground. So there it was, my room at the Ritz.

I was more miffed that the eight unchivalrous American men assumed that they were entitled to sleep under a roof while the Haitians slept outside than with sleeping outside myself. Patrick and Robinson, my gallant friends from Port au Prince, were not about to let me sleep outside alone, so they placed cots under the shanty's overhang.

As the sun descended to its own plywood cover in the sky, the eleven of us sat on homemade wooden chairs and swapped stories.

Mostly it was the Missourians' stories. Stories about bull-running in Spain, shark diving in South Africa, biking across the Sahara, and other manly things like that. I wasn't really paying attention. My mind was on my own inevitable vacation destination.

"Hey, Kim."

It was him again, the one who would be king.

"Got a sec?"

Seriously? No, I am very busy right now thinking of all of the things that are bound to crawl on me in the night—like snakes and tarantulas—and figuring out if my travel insurance will pay to have me airlifted out of the middle of nowhere to the nearest hospital with the right antivenin to keep me alive, or if I would have to channel Rooster Cogburn and suck it out.

"Sure."

"Hey, um, did you see the shower?"

Did I see the bedrooms? Did I see the shower? Buddy, what else is there to see? The only thing you haven't mentioned on these minuscule grounds is the latrine. Without a doubt, that was next.

"Yep."

The "shower" was a four-foot tall L-shaped wall in front of a fifty-five-gallon drum full of water. To take a shower, you fill a five-gallon bucket and then use a flimsy eight-ounce plastic cup to pour that water over your very sweaty, extremely dusty, likely smelly body, lather up, and rinse.

"I need you to do me a favor." Love, Kim, love. "I need you to shower last. We don't want the guys to be nervous that you might walk in on them."

There are so many things wrong with what he said. First, a favor? You can say no to a favor; I knew that I couldn't say no to his request. Walk in on them? How is that even possible? The wall is as tall as my eight-year-old grandson. I can see over the top of his head. Even in the pitch darkness, I would know that there was a figure in the "shower" and not have to walk around the corner to confirm my suspicions. Plus, I can count to ten. If one of them was missing, I might be able to do the math and know the missing guy is in the shower, since there is nowhere else to be except the latrine. I knew that one was coming too.

"Oh, and we will let you know when you are free to use the latrine."

Thank you, your majesty. How gracious and kind of you to let me, a lowly woman, graced by your radiant presence, sit on the same throne as thee. Love is patient and kind and whatever.

"No problem."

Sleeping Under the Plywood

By the time I was done showering everyone was either dreaming or snoring or both.

I ducked under the plywood onto the previously inflated air mattress and lay down. I then did what I did many times during that night and the nights to follow. I prayed. "Lord, please don't let anything with or without legs crawl on or anywhere near me."

By the end of hour one, my air mattress became an airless mattress, and I could feel every stone and stick underneath the deflated plastic. Also, in hour one and continuing through hour three I was serenaded by the delightful chorus of barking dogs and honking horns.

Hour four was relatively quiet. I drifted off to sleep, prepared to not jerk if I felt anything slither, crawl, or land on me.

Then came hour five. Voodoo drums started at some distance. Not exactly the calming roll of ocean waves, soothing sound of light rain, or gentle chirping of crickets, but the rhythmic percussion was surprisingly relaxing.

Just as I started to doze off to the pa rum pum pum pum, I heard the most gut-wrenching sound, one I had never heard before but knew exactly what it was. A dog was crying.

I have heard yelps, barks, whimpers, and howls of all kinds. I've witnessed dogs being kicked, stepped on, dropped, run over, and heard them voice their pain. This, however, was nothing remotely close to any of that. This bawling, a loud, long lament, an unearthly wail, made my heart sob. I wept quietly, prayerfully. *Lord! Please help that dog.* It seemed like an hour but was hopefully only minutes before the ungodly bellowing stopped. In rural areas of Haiti, hearing voodoo drums at night is not uncommon. Skinning a dog as part of a ritual, hopefully, is much less common.

The drumming eventually subsided and I was able to one-eye-open nap again. Deliverance came with the dawn.

After a day installing water filters in one-room shacks where families of four or more rested their heads at night, my private room with plywood covering my deflated mattress seemed like the Taj Mahal. I had nothing to complain about.

I got used to the routine of the night: enjoy the blow-up bed for a good part of an hour and then try to think of the rocks as a form of acupuncture, brace myself for the crying that proved certain to follow the beginning of the drumming, and pray over and over again, "Lord, please don't let anything crawl on me."

That night and the others that followed were similar to the first except for what happened the second night and two nights later.

Sometime between the drums ending and the sun rising above the horizon, my floating slumber came to an abrupt end when I felt something on my leg. Sleeping on my back, the best way to sleep if you might have to get up quickly to run, I was afraid to open my eyes. What if it's a snake? Do I jump up and risk a deadly bite? Do I pray that it is just there for a short visit and will slither on soon? What about a tarantula? I have seen many, always from a distance if they were alive. Dead ones I am willing to get closer to but not by very much. On mission trips I've taken kids tarantula hunting at night with flashlights, feigning bravery, secretly hoping that the spiders were all attending a family reunion in a town miles away. I dug down deep, found the last speck of courage hiding behind my spleen, and partially opened my right eye. I thought that if I only opened one, somehow whatever I saw would be half as scary. What if it was a chupacabra? I hadn't thought about that as a possibility until now. I know they are mythical, but so is bigfoot, and how many pictures of him are out there? I imagined a king-size hairless sphynx cat, the color of mud, fangs of a baboon, claws of a giant armadillo, lemur eyes, and spines protruding down its back. Did I really want to know?

I slowly lifted my head. Telling myself not to scream no matter what or how big it was, I opened my eye a bit wider, waiting for a monster to attack. Beady red eyes stared back at me while sharp talons gripped my thigh. Then I opened both eyes wide. Was I dreaming? No. The terrifying beast, the one that got my heart pulsing twelve hundred beats per minute like a pygmy shrew, raised my blood pressure well over stroke level, expanded my pupils to the size of vinyl records, and had sweat raining out of every pore causing a small flood on my deflated mattress was a chicken. A dang chicken. On my leg. I shooed the clucker away, knowing adrenaline would not let me sleep again.

Then two nights later, it happened again. Doing exactly the same things, squinting one eye, gradually bending my neck, imagining the worst and knowing I couldn't be that lucky twice, muscles tightened, ready to fend off an attack, and there it was again. The chicken.

That night, when dinner was served, I was comforted knowing there wouldn't be a three-peat. Sorry, old friend.

I really enjoyed getting to know the men of Missouri and chalked the whole thing off as a cultural difference. I clearly have different presumptions when it comes to the behavior of the sexes. I like a little help with my luggage and am happy for an opened door. Nothing crazy like throwing a trench coat over a puddle so I can cross the street, but a cot in a building would be nice.

So there it is, a record of wrong, something that love doesn't keep.

Changing the Memory Record

Love doesn't keep a record of wrongs, but that doesn't wash away our memories. We just look at the memories differently. Rather than letting bitterness take over, harboring angry feelings, wishing great bodily harm on someone you feel wronged by, the memory, the story, changes into just that: a memory, a story. Not keeping records of wrongs means the story no longer carries the emotion that it once did. It's no longer those dang Missourians who let me, made me, sleep outside with the chickens. Now it's just a funny story, a time in life that I will always remember, a time that I survived. I am stronger, braver, and smarter than I would be without experiencing life under plywood. I have more compassion for people who regularly sleep outside. Shoot, I can now sleep anywhere and know that I will be just fine. I really should be grateful to those pastors for making me live through those five nights in Arcahaie. They likely didn't know at the time what they were doing, but that doesn't matter. As with so many things in life, it is not what happens but our reaction to the happening. The narrative has changed, changed for the good and for good. The feelings that I had, before figuring out what love that doesn't keep a record of wrongs means, only hurt me. Those pastors never think about that time in Haiti as I do. Hopefully, their memory of the trip centers around the water filters that we installed and the families that welcomed us into their homes. The project launched that short week has continued, bringing clean water, water that does not make kids sick, into thousands of homes.

Recently, I ran into an old friend from high school. I told her that I have always felt bad about our graduation night. She and I had pooled our money for a bottle of sloe gin. (Man, I was cool in high school.) Somehow we ended up in different vehicles on the way to the bonfire on the beach. My car never made it. I ended up at a friend's cottage drinking half of the pint and maybe a beer or two, laughing all night as we swapped stories from our glory years. When I saw Ann the next day, she was not happy. I told her that we couldn't find everyone on the beach; Lake Michigan's shoreline is miles long, and everyone in my car had assumed that someone else would know where we were supposed to be. Unfortunately, we were all so excited for our big night of secret drinking that none of us bothered to ask. I handed Ann the half bottle of the red elixir. She insisted that she wanted her money back instead. I thought at the time that her insistence was ridiculous. I didn't get lost on purpose and there was no money. We spent it. But looking back, I realized that I should have refunded her two dollars and thirty-seven cents. What was she going to do with half a bottle of booze? Her parents would kill her if they found it in her room. I should have given her the money. The night of debauchery was over, never to get back. The sloe gin only held value that one special night.

Ann laughed. "Oh yeah, I remember that. I haven't thought about that in years! I was so mad. What was that? Like a buck fifty?"

She didn't think about it! Meanwhile, it was taking up a whole link on my guilt chain.

Ann knew love that kept no record. Things that are a big deal to us are just that, a big deal to us. Shortening my bulky necklace of shame felt good.

I remember a disagreement with my husband that turned into a full-blown blood-pressure-raising, adrenaline-pumping, voice-raising fight. Then when I finally convinced him of the error of his ways, or, more likely, he grew tired of an argument about nothing leading nowhere, he sighed heavily. "OK, OK, I'm sorry."

"You better be sorry! And while we are on the subject, two years ago, you forgot to take out the trash, and then there was that time that you didn't help empty the dishwasher in over a month. Do you have any idea how many diapers I have changed? Your son put a Matchbox car in the VCR." (He was my son too, but not right then.) "The VCR! I couldn't get it out, so I couldn't put a movie in for the kids. Have you ever mashed potatoes with a two-year-old on your leg? I am sick and tired of picking up your underwear off the floor. The hamper is six feet away."

I had such an epic rant going that I didn't even notice that Steve had moved to the couch and was watching college football.

I was the grand champion of keeping a record of wrongs. I could have gone on for hours. Instead, after I stomped away and my blood ceased its boiling, the argument seemed so trivial and foolish.

Love would have told me to can it, package it up, change the narrative, keep the story but in a whole different way, never to bring up in a grudge match again.

Lord, help me to see the wisdom of letting it go and loving without bad record keeping.

CHAPTER 10

LOVE DOES NOT DELIGHT IN EVIL BUT REJOICES IN THE TRUTH

WHO WOULD DELIGHT IN EVIL? That seems so clear: it is bad to delight in evil, yet we do, all too often, much more than we realize.

The seventeenth most-watched event in American history, after the moon landing, a bunch of Super Bowls, *M*A*S*H*'s final episode, and part eight of *Roots*, enraptured 95 million viewers, more than two and a half times the entire population of Canada. This event was the two-hour broadcast of a white Bronco motoring down a Los Angeles interstate, while the Knicks and the Rockets battled in game five of the NBA Championship. Domino's Pizza hit record sales during the two-hour broadcast. The YouTube video of Saddam Hussein's hanging received 19.4 million views, equating to the entire state of New York having a watch party.

We don't just watch; we root for failure. Heartbroken when we see Rodney King beaten or George Floyd choked, we react with disgust, anger, pity, but then watch it over and over again, retaliating by break-ing windows, destroying businesses, injuring many. We revel when others fall, watching over and over the agony of defeat, on the edge of our seats as verdicts are read, cheering over a sentence of life in prison.

So much do we savor the collapse, we forget anything good. Lance Armstrong fell hard, so hard that everything he accomplished beyond the doping scandal is forgotten. His incredible, unmatched cycling accomplishments, including seven consecutive Tour de France cham-pionships from 1999 to 2005, were all stripped away from him after his 2012 confession. With sponsors immediately canceling contracts, Armstrong lost $75 million in sponsorship income in one day. Nike cut all ties to Lance and Livestrong. All that he had fought for, all that he had done, was wholly taken away.

We forget about the good that Lance did before and don't recog-nize the good that he does now. After being diagnosed with metastatic testicular cancer in 1996, only twenty-five years old, and not given much hope, he found new treatments and survived, which led him to start the Livestrong Foundation in 1997 to help others going through cancer. It seemed like everybody had a yellow Livestrong bracelet. The message is still a source of strength to many dealing with cancer. That project raised $325 million for the foundation.

In 2005, Armstrong and a list of top athletes, including Andre Agassi, Muhammad Ali, and Mia Hamm, started a charity that finds opportunities for professional athletes to get involved in charitable causes. Athletes for Hope also encourages nonathletes to seek volun-teer opportunities and help in their own communities.

In 2006 he helped raise six hundred thousand dollars for Livestrong while running the New York City marathon. In 2009 he helped raise two million dollars for cancer research at the inaugural Pelotonia, a hundred-mile ride for charity in Columbus, Ohio. Although Lance is no longer involved, the foundation that he started in 1997 is going strong. Livestrong has supported more than eight million people through programs for cancer patients, survivors, and their families. Lance Armstrong's fall from grace changed his legacy of winning and giving and helping to cheating by using performance-enhancing drugs. Nobody talks about the good things, because we elect to delight in evil.

Delighting in evil is not just directed toward the famous. A lot of gossip is delighting in evil with sprinkles of envy. Spreading through town like poison ivy, broken marriages, money issues, and kids gone wild are hot topics. Even when told in confidence, stories too juicy just can't be contained. Imagine the stories heard by coffee shop walls. Gossip inflates a partial truth or outright false rumors, and it results in ruined reputations, divided families, and shattered friendship. Love does not gossip because love does not delight in evil.

Turn the record over, and there sits love rejoicing in the truth. The truth, the whole truth, and nothing but the truth. Truth is the unabridged story, the actual facts, no embellishment, no half answers. It is complete.

Partial truths are dangerous, often the cornerstone of a conspiracy. Just one person tweaking a story creates a viral sensation. Sightings of Elvis, Princess Diana, Michael Jackson, and Tupac are reported and then believed. Theories abound that Apollo Spacecrafts never landed on the moon, Big Pharma has a cure for cancer, and there was no Holocaust. And yet somehow five (four still visible) American flags made it to the moon. Thousands of people, people like us, would have to keep the cancer cure a secret. Surely at least one of them would let the cat out of the bag. Survivors of the Holocaust must despise that theory, having gone through agony, losing loved ones, then knowing some believe it never happened.

Partial truths sell papers. According to the tabloids, an alien bible was found, and they worship Oprah, a particular Jesus action figure heals the sick, and a husband's bad breath killed his wife. There are some fanatical Oprah fans, Jesus does heal the sick, and anyone's husband likely has bad breath from time to time. But love does not rejoice in partial truths; love wants the whole kit and caboodle.

Love not delighting in evil, yes. Love always rejoicing in the truth, I hope that is true of me.

Oh, Lord, help me.

Speaking the Same Language

Riding through Port au Prince is quite an experience. Cars, trucks, people, street vendors, colorful tap taps, motorcycles, brightly colored buildings, buildings with exposed cement blocks, UN Humvees, big black SUVs with dark tinted windows, dogs, goats, chickens (some clucking and some hanging upside down, skinned and covered in flies), huge pots boiling, horns, barks, music, yelling, laughing—it is a direct assault on all senses.

With my friend Kimberly along for support, Patrick and I headed down to the docks hoping for customs to release another container. Patrick, mostly patient, mostly showing love, likely got tired of our endless questions.

"Hey Patrick, when can we stop for cornmeal ice cream?" "How much longer before we get to port?" "How do you say 'give us our dang container' in Creole?"

"When we see a guy pushin' an ice cream wagon." "Ten minutes." "Kim, you can't say that to them."

Answers—mostly right, sometimes a guess, always stated as fact.

"Patrick, what is a bric-a-brac?"

One of the first questions I asked in Haiti was, "What is a Lesly Center?" Lesly Centers pepper the landscape like phone booths in the United States before pockets and purses took their place. I don't know who Lesly is, but he has a monopoly on all games of chance in Haiti. Numbers, soccer games, lottery, you name it, you can bet on it. Just like everywhere else, a buck can parlay a mason into a millionaire. Miniature structures with room for a stool, a cash box, and lots of cards, shutters opened on the street side, revealing chalkboards with the day's get-rich-quick opportunities. Like Lesly Centers, bric-a-brac shops are everywhere. This new question was long overdue.

"It's a porn shop."

"What! Are you serious?"

"Yeah, what's wrong with that?"

At that answer, Kimberly and I went from reasonably peaceful passengers to mutinous moralists.

"What's wrong with that? No money for food, gambling spots on every corner, and porn shops!"

"Why you guys so mad?"

"Because it's immoral. Shops like that in the United States are seedy, filthy places painted purple and with names like The Velvet Touch."

"Why's it bad?"

Why is Patrick not getting this? I know different cultures have different beliefs and customs, but this one is painfully, obviously wrong. Talk about delighting in evil. Women exploited, addictions created, marriages destroyed. While we have black cats, broken mirrors, and walking under ladders, Haiti has women who claim to be pregnant for years, yawning is taken as a sign of hunger, and picking up a baby from behind means that baby will never grow tall. Different strokes for different folks, but clearly, this should be a universal no-no.

And so our argument continued. Kimberly and I were yelling at dumbfounded Patrick. Patrick, a man who loves God, is faithful to his wife, and seemed to have a strong moral compass, is defending pornography. How can a guy in any culture who attends church weekly, prays daily, and walks uprightly, endorse such depravity? Who is this guy's pastor? Whoever he is, he is probably making women sleep outside.

Then it hit me like Babe Ruth's bat hit a baseball. Patrick was born in Haiti but moved to Connecticut when he was just a toddler, not moving back to Haiti until he was in his early twenties. He wasn't saying *porn*; he was saying *pawn*. Like when I ask him, "What do you call a small piece of land someone uses to grow vegetables?" just so I can hear him say, "A gahdin." Bric-a-bracs were pawnshops. Patrick was safe on first the whole time we thought he was out in left field. He was not delighting in evil—the revelation arrived just in time to pahk the cah at the yahd.

Experiencing the Evil of Poverty

New York City has residential buildings with as many as ninety-five floors reaching toward the sky with a population density of twenty-four thousand per square mile. Cité Soleil's eight square miles, with the majority of structures just one story above ground and the tallest structure being a cement block building reaching three stories, has a population density of thirty-one thousand per square mile. We think that New York sidewalks are over capacity, but they have nothing on Cité Soleil.

Cité Soleil was built on Port au Prince's largest garbage dump as a shanty town with housing for fifty-two families. In the overcrowded conditions, obtaining a census is much like counting marbles in a jar, but it is estimated that today somewhere between two hundred thousand and four hundred thousand call Cité Soleil home. Cité Soleil is known as the largest and most dangerous slum in the western hemisphere. During the day, Cité Soleil seems harmless, but self-preservation advises not to walk the streets at night.

There is a lot of poverty everywhere in Haiti, but Cité Soleil takes poverty to a whole other level. It is not uncommon to see children without shoes in Port au Prince. It is not unusual to see children with no clothes in Cité Soleil. In Port au Prince, the street vendors sit all day in the hot sun selling their wares. In Cité Soleil, the street vendors do not have to deal with just the hot sun, but if it rains, the market area floods, forcing street vendors to stand in mud in the hot sun. In Port au Prince, police are visibly present though not abundant. In Cité Soleil, they are neither visible nor present. When someone dies in Port au Prince, a car transports the body to a morgue. When someone dies in Cité Soleil, the body may just stay in the middle of the street.

The first time, the second time, the third time—I am not sure how many times—I rode through the streets of Cité Soleil, shock would run through my system. Besides dodging dogs and small children, the driver also had to steer away from a body, a body left out in the hot sun because no one had the means to move it anywhere else, or perhaps as an example. One time a man was caught robbing a house and shot in the back as he fled—and then left in the middle of the street for everyone to see what happens when you steal. Children threw small stones; older kids cursed and spat. Sure, stealing is wrong, but it doesn't warrant delighting in evil.

Patrick was as afraid of Cité Soleil as I am of chupacabras. Patrick was petrified. Over the years, I worked with several projects in Cité Soleil and asked Patrick to take me there. Quick with plausible rationale, he had to pay the customs broker, his truck needed air in the tires, his wife had a hankering for fish, endless reasons why he could not possibly join me in Cité Soleil. For years, he did everything and anything to avoid going anywhere near the place, as if Godzilla and King Kong lurked in the alleys ready to tear him and his truck to pieces.

With "people are people all over the world" as my slogan, I have never feared Cité Soleil. Just like anywhere in the world, a little street smarts go a long way. Don't go alone, never after dark, and hold on to your purse, just like New York subways in the 1980s. That is just walking in the truth.

As we made our way back to our accommodations after a long day, Patrick was in the driver's seat of a full eight-passenger van. As copilot and navigator, it was my job to keep our precious cargo, my good friends, safe and happy. It was also my job to show them my favorite places in Haiti. Seeing that we were on the main road that runs right past Cité Soleil, I thought I would try one more time.

"Come on, Patrick. It is a safe place."

"No way, you don't know what it's like in there."

"Really, because of everyone sitting in the front seat, I am the only one who has ever been inside, multiple times, pretty much every time I come to Haiti. But I don't know what it's like?"

"That's different."

Different how, because you are Haitian? Different because just the mere mention of Cité Soleil makes you shake like a twenty-five-cent vibrating bed? Different because the alley monsters won't attack me?

"It's not different; let's go."

"Not a good idea. We have people."

"Yep, I want to introduce these people to some of those people."

"It's gettin' late."

"Patrick. It is four in the afternoon."

"Everyone is hungry."

"Dinner is at six."

"I don't think we have enough gas."

"The tank is half full."

His excuses, my rebuttals—if he kept it up long enough, we would drive right by, and he would probably tell me that the van isn't capable of turning around.

Finally, Patrick gave in. "Fine."

Having never ventured in, Patrick was not familiar with the streets. His hands gripping the steering wheel like a vise, he steered left. Three men on the corner jumped up, waving their arms wildly, and they yelled something even Patrick didn't understand. Patrick kept turning. Others joined the three, more animated now than before.

"See Kim; these people are crazy!"

One man tried to get in front of the van to stop us. Patrick swerved to miss him. I didn't know what prompted all of the hubbub. Maybe they were just excited to see us and waving with extra gusto.

Adrenaline pushed his foot down farther on the gas pedal. We made it past the army of enthusiastic greeters, going a bit too fast into unknown territory. Then *bam!* Our speeding van came to a very abrupt halt. So did the tap tap directly in front of us that had been heading in our direction.

After a minute of disbelief, I said, "Where did he come from?"

"I don't know what happened. He came outta nowhere."

When I got out to survey the damages, the welcoming committee ran up yelling and pointing. I followed the pointer to a sign that read, "Sens unique." Putting up my hands in confusion led to more aggressive yelling and pointing.

"Patrick, what does that sign say?"

"One way."

"Oh." I guessed that the one way was not our way but the other way.

The tap-tap driver with just one passenger was furious, likely heading back toward home for the day. Patrick was a speechless ball of nerves. Our passengers were a little shaken but not injured.

Then the real show began. The crowd of a dozen or so pointing people grew to more than a hundred in minutes. People came from everywhere to see the wreckage and watch the fight. Delighting in evil, like watching a car crash anywhere. Except that car crash watchers where I live just slow traffic as they crane their necks from their vehicles. Here, craning necks isn't necessary. VIP seats are available all around.

Taking Responsibility

In Haiti, it is not about who is at fault. It is about who wins the argument—or fistfight, depending on how ugly things get. In this corner, weighing in at 210 pounds, the man from the van, the man who pays no attention to street signs, more powerful than a toy locomotive, able to leap over small puddles in a single bound, Petrified Patrick. And in this corner, weighing in at 140 pounds, driver of tap taps, madder than a rabid dog, fiercer than Beyoncé, tougher than he looks, The Guy. And the crowd goes wild.

Yelling, more yelling, chests pumping, adrenaline flowing, the two competitors stood toe to toe.

"Patrick, what is he saying?"

"Not now, Kim."

"Patrick, what do you want me to do?"

"I said, not now, Kim."

Man, he was in a zone, the ring.

"It's no big deal, you guys," I said to my friends in the van as if car crashes in Haiti were old hat to me. "They are just discussing terms."

It was a dance-off, and Patrick proved that he could have done pretty well on *American Band Stand*. The crowd grew even more massive and picked their favorite. Split pretty evenly down the middle, half cheering for Patrick and the other half booing him, delighting in the moment.

First, fault had to be established. It sure seemed like a no-brainer to me. A one-way sign pointed the wrong direction for Petrified Patrick to have much of a chance of winning round one. But fault took a while. Patrick finally conceded round one, after a gallant effort that tired his competitor.

Round two, the how-much-money round, started out hot. Words hitting hard with uppercuts and jabs, The Guy started high, Petrified Patrick went in low. The dance continued and then the bell rang. Round two was over. I was anxious to hear who triumphed.

Petrified walked back to his corner, where I was standing. "Give me fifty dollars." Fifty dollars, that's it? Nice. Patrick won the second round by a landslide.

"Fifty bucks?"

"Yeah, he wanted five hundred. I wore 'im out."

I quickly hand The Guy the money before he could change his mind.

"Kim, we have a problem." If I had a nickel for every time I heard Patrick say, "Kim, we have a problem," I would have at least ten dollars by now.

"Yes?" Now what? I thought the fight was over. What else was there?

Round three, I found out, involved a new, fresh opponent. The Guy, tap tap still functioning fine, was ready to drive away when his passenger entered the ring holding his head.

I looked for blood, a gash, a bump. As cornerman, I had remained outside the ring until now. As coach and the person holding the money, I thought I was justified in getting a closer look.

"He's not hurt. He just wants money." The boxer is now a doctor? It is entirely feasible that he hit his head when you drove into The Guy's grill.

"How much?"

"One thousand dollars."

"US?"

"Yeah."

"Holy cow." Fifty dollars for all of the damage done to The Guy's tap tap and a thousand dollars for this guy's not bleeding, gashed, or bumped head? The Guy was just the undercard. Passenger Man was the real contender, throwing a sucker punch and trying to turn

Petrified Patrick into a big palooka. Can't you do a little rope-a-dope or something?

Nobody moved or said a word for the three straight minutes during the stare-down portion of the show. Even the previously rowdy crowd fell silent, on the edge of their seats, waiting for the verdict.

I broke the silence. "Hey, you know Doctors Without Borders is right around the corner."

Without breaking the stare, Patrick said, "Yeah."

"Let's take him there." We need to walk the truth.

"Why?"

"Maybe he is really hurt. And we are the ones who hurt him." Really just you, but I did tell you to turn in.

After some quieter conversation, Patrick had the head-holding man sit in the front seat on our way to the small hospital in Cité Soleil. It was a slow start with many from the audience surrounding the van like paparazzi and mega fans trying to snap a picture or get a glimpse.

The small waiting room was empty when we entered. Just as the doctor was about to examine our boxer, another patient was carried in by two men. Surveying the new arrival's body from head to toe, I wondered what brought a guy like him into a place like this. Then I saw it. His foot. It was only partially connected to his leg.

I am well past getting woozy at the sight of blood. Raising kids, leading medical teams, coaching sports, I have seen enough to numb me up a bit. Blood, bone, and muscle, that's a horse of a different color. Breathing deep, trying hard not to become a patient myself, I turned around and grimaced at my friends. I wondered if they were seeing what I was seeing, but I'm not sure they had the same view because they were all the right color and I think I had turned to green.

The doctor wandered over and told us, after thirty seconds of looking in his eyes and asking a few questions, that our patient was fine. I'm thinking a little bump to the head doesn't really warrant much more attention when you've got a dangling foot on the other side of the room. I was rejoicing in the truth, grateful for the good news.

We dropped The Passenger off where he wanted, gave him fifty dollars, and headed home. A head and a grill sometimes have the same value in Haiti.

Praise the Lord, no one got hurt. My friends got a rare experience, one that they didn't see on the agenda, a bonus activity that they will always remember.

Fighting Discrimination

Beyond the evil of false assumptions and rumors, there are evil movements, governments, realities. Morally wrong or bad, wicked, harmful, injurious, and immoral—evil's defining words.

Evil is dangerous. Racism, discrimination, prejudices start wars, instigate violence, lead to murder. Subtler racism and discrimination overlook a job candidate because of the person's name, clutch a purse more tightly when a Black man walks by, or tell gay people that they are "not that gay," thinking it a compliment. Mistake a female physician for a nurse, assume an Asian student must be great at math, or presume a person of color is on the janitorial staff. Bank accounts, geography, education levels, positions, none are a definer of value. Yet people treated differently, judgments made, opportunities withheld are by-products of these prejudices. Turning backs on social injustices, blaming people for their poverty, or assuming unemployment equals laziness isn't love.

Videos of a man behaving badly prompted marches and protests across our country. In my city, what started out peacefully ended in a night of terror and destruction. Of the thousands who attended the peaceful protest, a hundred or so joined by others broke windows, ravaged shops, and destroyed property, leaving our downtown, like many others, in shambles. Early the following day, thousands flooded the streets with brooms, scrub brushes, and trash bags, many of whom were in attendance the night before and left before the violence started. These people, and many others, understood the marches as a way to bring change, not through destruction but through awareness.

With signs stating "Black Lives Matter," the message for the protesters, me included, is clear. Protesters may have been unaware and unsupportive of the organizational beliefs or actions, but they approve the message. When your life doesn't seem to matter as much as the next guy's, you want it known that you matter too. Not that he matters less, but you also do. Many find "all lives matter" offensive. Not because the statement isn't true, but because it fails to recognize the meaning of the message. Yes, all lives matter, but until all lives truly matter, in every way, without discrimination, then "all lives matter" is just words. "Blue lives matter," absolutely. "Black lives matter," unquestionably. "All lives matter," definitely. But until that statement works its way from the paper to hearts, until people realize that prejudicial challenges exist, until we work to tear down those barriers, inoculate discrimination, change isn't going to happen. Until someone has personal experience with racism, bigotry, prejudice, discrimination, it might be hard to see or believe.

As a woman in business and a nonprofit director, I don't really think about my gender until someone points it out to me. Regularly people stop by my office and ask to see my boss. If a male coworker is in the room, it is often assumed that he is in charge. Working in patriarchal countries, my gender closes more doors than it opens. Quite often, I have to pay more for services and work twice as hard to get paperwork through governments and gain the respect that is given to my male counterparts. Mostly I ignore the slights, but it doesn't mean they are not there. How much more do people face unfair treatment because of skin color or nationality?

Being part of a colorful family, my young granddaughters would be more excited to see what color their new little cousin would be than finding out the child's sex. Because color is beautiful. Any color should never be negative. We are just different shades of the same color.

Verse after verse, in both the Old and New Testaments, tell us that we are all equal, all created in God's image, all beloved.

Rejoicing in the Truth

Then there is the reverse of delighting in evil: rejoicing in the truth.

Love rejoicing in the truth has feet. This love wants to take action, not sit on the sidelines, ignoring the game. This love speaks out, stands up, supports. No passivity, but walking in truth, complete truth, even when it hurts, when there is a cost, when it affects your wallet, livelihood, or choice of friends. It is painful to see people living in poverty—children in ripped clothes getting inadequate nourishment, drinking contaminated water, sleeping on a dirt floor. But it is real. Opening your eyes hurts. It is so much easier to disregard than to see. Giving from your billfold costs. Living love that rejoices in the truth compels you to feed the hungry, provide water to the thirsty, and visit the sick.

Giving of yourself, volunteering to help those in need, taking a stand for justice, speaking up when rumors, racial slurs, or condemnations are in earshot—that's boots-on-the-ground love that rejoices in the truth. Put your money where your love is. Think before you speak. Listen with love that is patient. Find the truth about what is offensive, what makes someone feel less. Drop the prejudices. See and love the individual. Love that rejoices in truth never looks away.

Love rejoicing in truth grows, changes. As we grow and change, truth reveals, not all at once but little by little. Eugene Peterson in *The Message* calls this the "flowering of truth" (1 Cor. 13:6). I love that. I see forgiveness in that. I believe differently than I did when I was twenty or thirty or forty. By walking in love that rejoices in the truth, I am discovering truth. I appreciate friends who speak truth into my life, call me out on things, help me see from a different angle.

The whole truth is that the accident was our fault. We walked in that truth, not as quickly as we should have, but Haiti has special car accident protocol. Our flowering of the truth happened after a duel. But truth flowered all the same.

Lord Jesus, help. Open my eyes that I would not buy into what is evil. Help me to crave, seek, thirst for truth, the truth that love rejoices in. Help me to know when truth needs to triumph over culture more quickly.

CHAPTER 11

LOVE ALWAYS PROTECTS

LOVE ALWAYS PROTECTS. IT GUARDS against attacks, keeps the bully on the other side of the playground. Love shields from harm, throws an arm in front of the passenger while slamming on the brakes. It defends, speaks up when insults are hurled. It shelters from danger, makes it safe inside during a thunderstorm. It's got your back. It is Secret Service love, "worthy of trust and confidence."

Losing Steve stinks, but I have never been angry or begrudged him. He was the guy who would get up at 5 a.m., read the Bible, read a devotional, and pray. He pursued God. Not ebbing and flowing, just a straight-line trajectory, always moving forward and up. He got to go to heaven a little early. Good for him—he finished strong. Stinks for me, but I am truly happy for him.

My dad stepped in as protector. We were really close before, but we got even closer after Steve died. My dad did that not just for me but for my kids. All are now grown, but everyone needs someone to turn to for advice and wisdom.

My dad helped my youngest, Noah, and his wife, Susie, move to Dallas, Texas, in the middle of July. Noah, starting his PhD in cancer biology a week later, found a condo near UT Southwestern at a reasonable lease price. Actually, Susie is more likely the one who found it. Susie lives love that always protects Noah. On the third floor with no elevator in 104-degree heat, my dad helped carry up every bit of content from the U-Haul.

He fixed things at my daughter's house, helped her get through some tough times, and always assured her safety. He attended first Noah's and then Luke's Navy boot camp graduations. As a former sailor, he burst with both pride and tears. He and Paul spent a lot of time together and became so close that he was Paul's obvious choice for best man. He relished touring NASA with Luke, so proud of Luke's work. With such a close relationship, my dad often forgot that my daughters-in-law, Megan and Susie, were not my offspring. He adored my grandbabies almost as much as I did.

My dad was always a phone call away, there when I needed him, there just to be there. I talked to him nearly daily and saw him as much as life allowed.

He was so full of life, my aunt Barb used to joke that he was like the Energizer Bunny, just kept going and going. His recipe for a long, healthy life consisted of half a banana and some oatmeal every morning and a glass of red wine at night. He loved deeply, his wife, her kids, his kids, grandkids, family, friends, and neighbors. Always willing to lend a helping hand. Always ready to give the shirt off his back, typically flannel.

He loved and pursued God. Attended mass every morning with his brother Bill, helped Father Jose with maintenance at his aging church, fixed appliances for shut-ins, or bought them a new one if it was just too old to fix. He dedicated many hours to Rays of Hope, worked in Haiti and the Dominican Republic.

Thinking he was going to outlive us all, it was shocking to discover his beloved Navy gave him a gift. After he slept directly under asbestos for years, developing mesothelioma was just a matter of time. For the six weeks between his diagnosis and heaven, my brothers and I tag-teamed staying with him at home, because he needed extra help, especially at night. I tried to take the lion's share to be with him for as long as I could.

Losing him was devastating.

After Steve died, I still had my own cancer stuff to deal with, and as soon as that was over, I took a position as a part-time bookkeeper at Rays of Hope. Twelve days later, an earthquake in Haiti killed tens of thousands of people, leaving the country mourning and devastated. I flew to Haiti two weeks later, then again nearly every month for the next several years. I hit the ground running. I did not take time to grieve Steve.

The months after losing my dad were some of the hardest of my life. I couldn't think clearly, I forgot things, I had no focus. I was living in a fog. I had never taken the time to deal with losing Steve, and adding my dad's loss was like a double whammy. On top of that, I had just ended a relationship that went south in a hurry.

Never having gone to a counselor before, I was apprehensive but knew what I had to do. I asked around, got a number, called it, and got a voice mail back. The counselor had no room for new patients but had a recommendation, a woman named Bennett. Right away, I called and left a message.

A couple of hours later, my phone rang.

"Kim?"

"Yes."

"This is Denise Bennett. Why do you want to see me?"

Not what I was expecting to hear. Nothing like getting right to the point.

"Well, where to start. Um, I was diagnosed with breast cancer a few years ago."

"Oh, no. Are you OK?"

"Yeah, I'm fine. But four months later, my husband was diagnosed with pancreatic cancer."

"No way." She's a little casual. Maybe that's a good thing.

"It was hard. He died six weeks later."

"Oh, I'm so sorry."

"He was an awesome guy. I probably had it better than most people do their whole life. And heaven is a great place." My standard three-sentence answer to "I'm so sorry."

"It still has to be hard."

"Yes, well, then I recently lost my dad."

"Oh, no."

"We were really close."

"I'm so sorry."

"He was a great guy, an awesome dad, wonderful to my kids."

"Sounds like a great man."

"For sure. Then I just broke up with someone who messed with my head."

"Oh, dear."

"I know. I think he is a sociopath, for real, like a textbook case."

"Yikes."

"I haven't done such a great job of dating since losing my husband."

"Sounds rough."

"Yeah, so, I thought it might be a good idea to talk to someone."

"That is a good idea."

"I just want to make sure that I'm not attracting sociopaths, like someone in a Lifetime Movie."

"You probably should talk to someone."

"I never have before, so this is pretty new to me."

"It will probably be really good for you."

"I guess so."

"I'm a little confused, though." She's the counselor and she's saying she's confused—is that a bad sign?

"About what?"

"I'm your son's landscaper, and he told me to give you a call."

"Oh my gosh, I'm so sorry."

"No, no, don't be."

"I'm so sorry; I was expecting a call."

"It's OK, really."

"You are so sweet."

"I promise I will never tell anyone."

I laughed. "You can tell whoever you want because I will be telling this story."

My son was in the middle of building a house and a little overwhelmed. Denise Bennett, not the counselor Bennett, was working on his yard. I told him to have her call me to take something off his plate.

She doesn't even know me, or maybe now she knows me a little too well, and she is showing me love that protects. Without hesitation, she wanted to protect me from embarrassment—what a kind soul.

Upgrading the Hospital Room

With high school mission teams from the United States, a regular evening activity in Los Alcarrizos, Dominican Republic, is playing basketball at the end of a long day of shoveling dirt and laying blocks. Lighthouse Projects hosted our fifty-four students from a Christian school in my hometown and a handful of adult chaperones. On their grounds is a pretty nice outdoor court with bleachers for any spectators or nappers.

The best Dominican players from the school, along with Cristian (who is the best in the world, just ask him), and members of the missions team talk smack and play ball.

I love to go watch but that evening I had to take care of some paperwork, so I didn't see what incited the screams. Running down, afraid of what I was about to see, I didn't take any time to worry about stepping on snakes or other vermin in the brush and just forged ahead in my flip-flops.

A group had gathered in a circle, all looking down.

"What's going on?"

"It's Chad." Love always protects and I was not there to protect him.

"What happened?"

"He tried to dunk."

Chad, a highly skilled, five-foot-eight point guard, was lying flat on his back on the concrete court.

Witnesses said Chad ran, then jumped, catching the rim like a gymnast grabbing the horizontal bar. The momentum of his mount caused his feet to swing forward, making his body parallel to the ground beneath. His legs then swung back to an equal height the other way; the backswing initiated his dismount. Falling from the full height of the ten-foot basket, failing to stick the landing, his face made the initial contact, and the impact knocked him out.

Kids, tools, and construction; separate from each other, nobody gets hurt. Put the three together, and you might need a med kit. Over the years, there have been some cuts, twisted ankles, pulled muscles, dehydration, bumps, and bruises, all happening on the worksite.

A kid injured while attempting to dunk a basketball, this was something new.

Chad came to by the time Cristian pulled up in a cargo van. After cautiously moving him onto a mattress, carefully setting the bed in the back of the van, Chad's makeshift ambulance headed to Santo Domingo. Fortunately, Cristian got in touch with a local doctor who sat on the floor by Chad's injured head and tended to him the entire drive. Chad's friend Ryan, Greg (another adult from the group), and I filled the rest of the space.

Parking for emergency vehicles was across the street from the hospital. Cristian ran in for help. Soon two men watched for traffic, then wheeled a gurney to the van. Instead of the usual white sheet, the mattress covering was a blood-stained lilac floral bed linen, perfect for a little girl's room.

Again after we waited for traffic to clear, Chad's bed on wheels made it over the bump and curbs into the *sala de emergencias.*

There was a lot of talk before any action. Cristian, our doctor, and two ER docs discussed Chad's situation in rapid Spanish. They may have chatted about their families, the weather, and major league baseball games, hard to tell.

Blood work first, Chad brave, Ryan nearly fainting.

On the ride there, Ryan stayed pretty quiet verbally, but his face was screaming. Eyes wide open, jaw slacked, and ghost white, he looked like a wax figure from The Hollywood Horror Museum.

We were happy to know the hospital had a CAT scan machine, and soon Chad, followed by his supporters, was wheeled down the narrow hall for the test. The doctor conducting the test invited us all in to watch. Ryan and I stayed by Chad for moral support. Greg viewed the screen, ready to give his diagnosis.

"Great news, Chad!" Greg said. "You have a brain."

Blood work, physical exam, and X-ray were handled more privately. Ryan and I waited in the hallway. With Ryan leaning on a door leading to who knows where and me leaning on the wall next to him, we had a full sight of the hospital lobby.

Ryan finally found his voice while maintaining the scream. "This place is freaking me out."

"It's not bad." Top-notch compared to others I have visited. Trying to calm his nerves a bit, I decided to start a conversation. "So, how's baseball?"

"Fine."

"How's the season look?"

"Fine."

"How do you think the Tigers will do this year?"

"Fine."

"A clown is standing behind you with a butcher's knife."

"Fine."

So much for conversation.

Staying far away from the ER and possibly faint-inducing blood, we watched the comings and goings of visitors.

A taxi the size of a Ford Escort pulled up to the front entrance. Two men got out and walked right toward us. Horrified, Ryan and I stepped out of the way. The door that Ryan had been leaning on was their target destination. For a minute, Ryan thought he was going to lose a kidney.

Standing upright in the closet was an adult-size baby-blue coffin. The men laid the coffin down right beside us and opened the lid. I grabbed Ryan's arm to keep him from falling. Relief in seeing it empty was just a fleeting moment as two more men came out of nowhere carrying the body of a petite older woman. Now both of us were wide-eyed and slack-jawed. They gently placed Grandma Moses in the empty box and closed the lid. Each taking a corner, they lifted the casket, holding it like a waterlogged tree. They must not know the shoulder trick. Neither of us dared to blink as we watched the pallbearers walk across the lobby and through the front doors. They waited for the taxi driver to open the trunk. Tilting the baby-blue box to a forty-five-degree angle, they slid her in. With the hatch wide open and half of the sarcophagus hanging out, the men got in and drove away.

Ryan and I looked at each other in utter disbelief. I love Ryan and am not doing such a great job protecting him from danger and scary things.

"Did that just really happen?"

"I think so," I said.

"I was leaning on that closet door."

"The casket was empty then."

"There was a casket behind the door I was leaning on."

"It's just a wooden box."

"For dead people."

"Yep."

"I'm freaking out."

There we go again. This time I won't ask about baseball.

The doctors, though very optimistic, worried about a concussion and admitted Chad for the night.

Greg dreaded calling Chad's folks to let them know what happened. After the doctor's good report, the phone call was much easier.

The phone rang twice, then Chad's dad answered.

"Hey, Dave, this is Greg." That might scare any parent to get a phone call from a person in charge of your son far from home.

"Is everything OK?"

"Chad's fine, really, but he is staying in the hospital overnight." Not what he wanted to hear.

"Oh no, what happened?"

"Well, see, he was trying to dunk a basketball and . . ."

"He was trying to dunk a basketball?" Chad's dad was flabbergasted. Maybe it was not something he ever expected Chad to attempt. Dave was happy to hear that Chad was fine but laughed a little at how he got hurt.

After the phone call, Cristian and Greg left to find food while Ryan and I got Chad settled.

A hospital bed, striped sheets this time, filled the space that was smaller than an inside cabin on the Love Boat. Windowless and spinach green, it thankfully had a private bathroom. Not so thankfully, a hook held a dirty, used towel hung next to a pair of plaid boxers, likely also dirty and used. Neither the room nor the lavatory had seen a mop, sponge, or soap for quite some time.

I thought, *For just one night, it's tolerable, so long as nobody touches anything.*

Chad kept his cool until Ryan told him about the scene in the lobby. All of a sudden, Ryan was full of words, expounding on every detail. Chad didn't look too happy to be hearing about it.

A nurse interrupted the animated storyteller and motioned for Chad to get out of bed, then sent the three of us into the hallway. She shoved Chad's bed tightly against the wall and then another nurse helped her move a second bed into the already tight space. The beds wedged together were like Ricky's and Lucy's nine months before meeting Little Ricky.

Oh no, not a roommate. The room was terrible enough; Chad sleeping side by side with a stranger just could not happen.

"Is there another room available?"

The woman behind the desk prickled at my question.

"No. Full."

Turning back to the boys, my eyes caught the elevator door opening. Like fraternity brothers getting out of a phone booth, people kept coming out of the elevator. Eighteen years old or so, the face of the young man on the stretcher was more battered than Chad's after he fell on his face from ten feet above the ground. Both eyes bruised and swollen, lips cut open, scrapes and scratches everywhere. One leg had a compound fracture that had not yet met a surgeon. A neck brace, one arm in a sling—whoever did this to him didn't leave much for anyone else.

Eight family members accompanied this bundle of hurt, the women wringing their hands and crying, the men talking loudly using big hand gestures. One was on his cell phone, talking to the police.

Please take him down the hall. Please take him down the hall, I kept repeating, hoping that if I wished it enough times, it would happen.

No such luck. Battered boy moved into Chad's room for a sleepover.

To make matters worse, Chad's roommate's beating came from rival gang members who promised to finish the job in the hospital.

Lord Jesus, can't we love this kid from down the hall?

"Please, is there a different room?" I asked again.

"No. Full."

I called Cristian and told him that Chad could not be killed by some Dominican gang. His folks would like us to bring him home alive. He had to do something. Handing my phone over to Nurse Full, I prayed for a miracle. After a chat, she handed the phone back.

"Cristian, they have to have another room! Chad can't stay here."

"Mamma, I . . ."

"I am serious. I think the kid's whole family plans on spending the night with him."

"Mamma, just . . ."

"Cristian, I mean it. If he stays here, he is leaving in a baby-blue box." I love Chad and love always protects. Find a room!

"What?"

"Never mind."

"Mamma, I got him a room." Why didn't he say so in the first place?

"Great, you are amazing. Thank you. Where? We need to go."

"It's on the floor for rich people."

"Huh?"

Hospitals in many countries, including the Dominican Republic, have different floors for the rich and the poor. While poor people stay in dirty, crowded rooms, floors for the wealthy have spacious accommodations, more nurses, meals included, color TV, and air-conditioning.

"The only thing is you have to pay more money."

"No problem." Chad's moving. "How much?"

"I'm not sure." I did not care how much it cost to save Chad's life while sleeping next door to Alex Rodriguez.

As promised, the wealthy floor was beyond beautiful. Gorgeous mahogany covered the walls, hand-laid tiles covered the floors, and Spic and Span visited daily. Even the nurses dressed differently, crisp white dresses, white nylons, and shoes.

On one side of Chad's sizeable private room, a big bed with extra pillows, a nightstand, two chairs, and a color TV still left plenty of open space. A sofa, two more chairs, a coffee table, end tables, and another color TV served as a sitting area on the other side of the room.

Chad's spacious bathroom complete with walk-in shower was not only spotless but there were no dirty towels or used boxers.

Greg and Ryan spent the night with Chad.

Before Chad was released happy and alive the next day, we had a bill to pay.

I was adding things up in my head: CAT scan, X-ray, blood work, pain medicine, private room, and more. In the United States, just the overnight stay averages ten thousand dollars. Add on a few grand for a CAT scan, and however much for everything else, if the prices were even half that much in Santo Domingo, I would be the one selling Ryan's kidney.

Cristian and I went to the business office to settle up. A kind woman punched numbers from a small pile of papers into her calculator. She double- and then triple-checked. My stomach was churning, but Chad was alive. His girlfriend, Kate, was especially happy about that.

She finished and handed me a paper with the total. The number on the paper was 18,922.96. What! Where's Ryan? I might need both kidneys.

"Mamma, that's pesos."

Praise the Lord, thank you, Jesus! I paid 323 US dollars. Ryan's kidney is safe.

Training in Self-Protection

Love always protects. Of course, we can't protect kids from getting hurt during a basketball game. Kids at play are going to scrape knees, get stitches, and break a bone. Protecting a kid from all of that is not love; it's smothering, limiting growth and independence. However, "Chad, since you are five eight, have never dunked before, and have been hauling cement blocks all day, now might not be the time to make your first attempt" could indeed be love that protects.

Deeper than that, protective love stands up, speaks out when something hurtful is said or a lie is spread. Love that always protects offers shelter in a storm, whether weather storms or the hardest times. Not running away but staying behind to help, to protect. It stays if things seem sketchy, if there is a chance of harm. It pushes trouble out of the way, guarding against attacks.

Like with Chad. I would have done anything to make sure that he was safe from harm, any harm, and that he was physically OK. As with love in general, there can be a cost, but the cost cannot be a consideration. No matter what it takes, what sacrifices you have to make. Money, time, and comfort are all things that protective love is willing to surrender. Love loves people. Every person is worth more than any amount of money, time, or comfort.

Protecting reputations, love does that. Love that always protects does not listen to lies without speaking truth. It does not laugh in order to be part of the crowd. It does not buy into idle gossip. It speaks out.

Love also protects those you love from themselves. Self-doubt, giving up, not recognizing value—these are harms love always protects against.

Love that always protects, protects against all harms.

I wanted to protect my son Paul and his friends when they were bullied in middle school. A boy who grew tall and strong before the rest waited in the bathroom for his next swirly victim. He called names, pushed, punched, spat, and did all kinds of mean things, always out of the teacher's view.

Every day Paul begged not to have to go back to school. I agreed and wanted to protect him because I love him. I cried thinking of the torment my son had to endure. I did not want him ever bullied again. I wanted to keep him safe, protected at home. Steve disagreed; he did not believe keeping him home was the way to protect him. We fought. I fought for my son, believing that the only way to protect him was to keep him out of harm's way. Steve won the battle, promising to teach Paul how to box. After dinner each night, he took Paul to our base- ment workout area, trained him to lift weights, and taught him how to hit. Steve told Paul that he was never to throw the first punch, but if he was hit, "hit back and don't stop until someone pulls you away." Paul started gaining confidence, something that can be a bully repellent. Braver and stronger, he was preparing to fight back if he had to.

At work one day, I received a phone call from Paul's gym teacher.

"You need to come and get Paul."

"Is he OK?"

"He's fine, but he is suspended from school for the next three days."

"What?" Noah maybe, but never kind-hearted, sweet, never-get-in-trouble Paul.

"For the next three days, you give Paul whatever he wants, ice cream, pizza, take him to the movies, whatever he wants to do."

"Huh?"

"That boy, the bully, didn't like a call during kickball and pushed Paul. Paul hit back. Paul ended up on top of him, hitting him over and over. I walked to where they were as slowly as I could, then pulled Paul away. I was so proud. You should be too."

Love that always protects isn't always a helicopter mom; sometimes it's a let-me-teach-you-something-that-will-help-you-in-life kind of dad.

Love that always protects can look different than you think. It is not always standing up to the bully for the bullied. Sometimes it is teaching the bullied how to stand up for himself, protecting him from a lifetime of bullies.

Love doesn't protect against a failing grade by doing the homework. It lets the failure happen, protecting from a lifetime of dependence.

Love that always protects doesn't protect from a car accident by never handing over the keys. Love instills confidence, work ethic, and wisdom, which protect the ones you love when you are not there to do it yourself.

Protective love doesn't blame the teacher, coach, or boss. Love that always protects recognizes that blaming others for failure can stifle growth. Instead, it protects those we love from future harm by helping them learn and grow from life's situations.

Praying about what love means makes it clearer all the time. I want to protect the right way all the time.

Lord Jesus, help me to see when and how to love the love that always protects. Help me not keep my mouth or wallet closed when they need to be open to protect others. Help me to know that sometimes love that always protects, protects differently than expected, perhaps in a basement weight room.

CHAPTER 12

LOVE ALWAYS TRUSTS

LOVE TRUSTS. TRUST IS FRAGILE, like a Fabergé egg, exceptionally delicate and extremely valuable, but if you drop it, it breaks into a million pieces. Gluing those pieces back together can take years, a lifetime, if you can put it back together at all.

Trust is rarely automatic. A nun sporting a habit is one of the exceptions. Every story you have ever heard about nuns in Catholic schools is true. The stories might grow like a caught fish over time, but true. Nuns are scary, rulers-on-knuckles kind of scary. The kind of scary that makes you sit up straight, turn in all of your homework, and not talk during class. Three critical things to know in a nun's classroom are chewing gum is like a cow chewing its cud, a messy desk is the devil's playground, and if a Sister tells you to jump, you don't ask how high without raising your hand first.

Even though I was completely intimidated by her, I trusted Sister Mary Louise from the first moment I saw her. A woman of girth, much taller than any middle schooler, just her presence in the building put you on notice. Her presence in your presence struck fear deep into your being, killing any bravery stock that had accumulated in your soul bank.

At the end of my Catholic school years, with eighth-grade graduation just a couple of days away, I witnessed the most extraordinary
phenomenon, rarer than a unicorn sighting or catching the Loch Ness
monster on film. When told that he must clean his desk that instant,
Fred, my classmate, told Sister where she should go, and it was not a
place where harps are played. At that moment, all breathing and heart
beating ceased. The clocks died, the earth stopped revolving, and all
the angels said, "Huh?"

I couldn't move my head to watch him stomp out of the classroom
from fear that I might turn to stone. I knew it was highly likely that
Fred would never be seen again, not by us, not by his family, not by
anyone. I had no idea what was going to happen but imagined a leather
belt, fire, and eternal damnation would be in the mix.

The rest of the day, the whole school, maybe the whole world, was
quieter than Microsoft's Building 87 research lab, where it is said that
noise goes to die. Not a word was spoken, all sneezing and coughing
were suppressed, and sighs took a hike. Even the bus ride home was
silent as we all knew that no one could ever hear about this unspeak-
able incident, especially our parents, who might think that we were
guilty by association.

The next day the classroom fell silent again when Fred, rising from
the dead, entered and walked straight over to his desk like it was just
another day. The bell was a few minutes away from ringing when
Sister Mary Louise summoned me to her desk. With her sitting and
me standing, we were looking eye to eye.

She whispered, "When class starts, I want you to raise your hand,
stand up by your desk, and ask if I am going to let Fred graduate with
the class."

The walk back to my desk was like walking the green mile. First,
we never, ever stood when we asked a question, so how awkward was
that! Second, Fred was my friend, so how could I be the one to put him
in the hot seat? But Fred already told Sister where to go and I wasn't
about to remind her of his suggested destination. I just had to obey.

The bell rang and I raised my hand. "Yes, Kim."

I stood. "Sister, are you going to let Fred graduate with our class?" There, I did it. It was over—such a relief. Before I could sit back down, I heard Sister say, "Well, I don't know. What do you think, Kim?" *What do I think? You didn't tell me I had to think!* I think I wish I had the flu and had called in sick. I think that you are putting me on the spot, a spot that I did not create. I think that if I say the wrong thing, I will end up gnashing teeth with Fred. I think I might faint.

Thinking about everything except the words to say, I said, "Sister, Fred is our friend." Yikes! I called the devil my friend. My parents are going to be getting a phone call very soon.

"Hmm. What do the rest of you think?"

Ah, the pressure was gone. I was out of the spotlight. Annie, bless her heart, raised her hand, and said a few words. Others chimed in. Sister relented and gave Fred permission to attend graduation.

Even that did not break my trust. Even though Sister Mary Louise caught me off guard, made me do something unprecedented, I still trusted her. Sister Mary Louise never lied, not about life lessons, chewing gum, or how to diagram a sentence. Never telling a lie must be one of the vows novices take before entering full sisterhood, right behind poverty and chastity.

Breaking Trust

Breaking trust rips at your gut. I will always remember the time I was supposed to babysit and stayed at my cousin's instead. Mrs. Romkema trusted me to be there. Knowing that I broke that trust felt horrible. It still feels horrible. I was never asked to babysit for that family again. I lost not just their trust but their respect. That hurts too.

My worst breaking of trust, breaking beyond all breakings, gold medal, MVP, Oscar winning breaking happened in seventh grade. I was cool, part of the in crowd (if there is such a thing in a class with twenty-six students). My coolness was affirmed by doing cool things with cool people. So cool that I felt the need to write about my coolness in a diary. I swore, talked about smoking, boys, and how much I hated my period.

Normally tucked under my mattress, I mistakenly left the impressive memoir on the kitchen counter one Saturday. Calling home from a 4-H event, I was greeted with "We read your diary." If there is anything that will knock you off the coolness pedestal, it is your parents reading about it. I knew that they would not find me cool. My world came to an abrupt halt. The earth stopped spinning, the skies darkened, and air got so heavy it was hard to breathe. I knew two things. First, I was in big trouble. I knew I had seen the last of the outside world, that I would be grounded forever. Second, I broke their trust.

Banished to my room after a good talking-to, wondering if I would ever be let out again, I thought about all of the ways that I hurt the people who gave me life.

So love trusts. But not just trusts sometimes but "always trusts." So, where does that put trusting a nun or losing my parents' trust? Maybe there is a whole different kind of trust that loves.

Trustworthy Leadership

Dion DiMucci, a pop singer turned Christian artist in the 1960s and '70s, sang a song that still plays in my head sometimes. "Trust in the Lord" is based on something that Solomon wrote many moons ago. "Trust in the LORD with all your heart and lean not on your own understanding; in all your ways submit to him, and he will make your path straight" (Prov. 3:5–6). His lyrics are a tad paraphrased but nearly Solomon's words verbatim. In the song, Dion sings about Daniel in the lions' den, Jonah getting along in the belly of a whale, and Abraham being called to sacrifice Isaac, all trusting in the Lord with their whole hearts. When in the same room with lions, stuck in the belly of a fish, or walking your son to his death, trusting for a good outcome takes some true grit. The way Eugene Peterson's *The Message* interpreted this passage is, "Trust GOD from the bottom of your heart; don't try to figure out everything on your own. Listen for GOD's voice in everything you do, everywhere you go; he's the one who will keep you on track." From the bottom of your heart, trust then listen for the most direct route to your destination.

Trustworthy Love

OK, Haiti, with your curvy roads, it's learning time.

I brought a group of medical students from Central Michigan University to OSAPO, Oganizasyon Sante Popilè / People's Health Organization, a medical clinic created and run by Dr. Gardy. Dr. Gardy lived on the streets as a boy. A compassionate American paid his elementary and high school tuition, enabling him to go on to medical school. He studied in Haiti, the United States, and Germany, and now serves about thirty thousand people in rural areas around Rousseau, north of Port au Prince. Gardy trains and supervises community health workers and midwives who go to areas where health care is otherwise nonexistent. He also has an HIV clinic, prenatal and nutrition center, maternity ward, water purification and distribution system, latrine program, huge farm, lots of chickens, and a massive heart. Gardy is adventurous, funny, and a little unpredictable. He is also very respected, loved, and trusted. If anywhere with anyone, I should be able to discover love that trusts here.

The students, every single one of them amazing people, could not wait to help in any way they could. Dr. Gardy arranged for us to operate a day clinic near the top of a mountain. With no transportation, living in such a remote area makes it difficult for people who need medical attention to make it all the way down to his clinic, harder still the return trip back up.

The early morning ride up was a little harrowing for some on curvy, one-lane dirt roads that sometimes pretended to be two, with no guardrails, edged in steep drop-offs. Because the driver knew these roads like he knew his momma, I trusted him and love dhim, because love trusts.

After a full day of seeing patients, I let him know that not everyone was so keen on going back down the same way we came up, so Gardy said, "Let's walk," and immediately started a caravan down the mountain. I held back to make sure we had everyone. Clearly the doctor, who took off like a drag racer, trusts me to do the counting; he must love me.

Ahmad had a prosthetic leg as a result of boyhood cancer, making the hike difficult, but he was willing to brave the truck ride. Dahlia was using the hole-in-the-ground ladies' room when Gardy exited, and she really wanted to walk back. I waited for her, and then Dahlia and I set off to catch up.

Right away, we came to a bend in the road. From the drive up, I pictured the road as a zigzag of switchbacks. Being an experienced mountain climber (I did win King of the Hill once in fifth grade), it made sense to me to take a shortcut through the trees so we could meet up with the road where we would find Gardy and the group. Dahlia was game so down we went. Then down farther into more trees, then more. I thought the road would have shown up, but it never did. We reached a massive open area and looked everywhere for a sign of life, but looking produced nothing. We were all alone on a big mountain. What did Dahlia think when she trusted me? What was I thinking? Why did I trust me?

"We can do this. We don't need them."

We started walking again, and two young girls came up behind us. I wished I had worked harder to learn Creole.

"Sa wout la?" Is the road there? I pointed.

Giggles, all I got were giggles. I guess they never run into strangers in their back yard, particularly a fifty-something white woman with a twenty-year-old Indian girl. That and my Creole might have been wrong or completely incomprehensible.

"OSAPO? Rousseau la?" Pointing again.

More giggles, great. Maybe not tour guides.

The girls motioned us to go in the opposite direction of our current course, so we waved and continued on. They ran ahead of us and then motioned some more for us to go back up. Since we were going down and we didn't speak the same language, I waved again, said, "Mesi," and kept on trucking. Keeping the ocean to our left meant we would eventually arrive somewhere down there. Turning around would put our watery compass on the wrong side. My inner compass would just not allow it.

With all of this time together, we really got to know each other. Dahlia is a delight. As a first-generation American, attending medical school was honoring to her grandfather. He had always wanted to be a doctor, but because of the caste system in India, he was a holy man. Graduating from high school early and then earning her bachelor's degree in just two and a half years gave Dahlia the position of youngest in her med school class. Old enough to vote but too young for tequila. So smart, so sweet, and so trusting. Love trusts.

Early in our hike, I apologized for getting us into this situation. Dahlia smiled and said she loved an adventure and that this was a great one. Fabulous attitude. I'll take it. Every hour or so, I apologized again and Dahlia just smiled, reminded me that this was something she would always remember, and trusted me to get us home alive. Poor naive girl.

Parts of our walk were fairly steep. We learned quickly that sliding down the sandy mount beat falling down the sandy mount. Before long, we became world-class sand surfers, her in her Nikes and me in my Sketcher sandals with a two-inch heel, maybe not the best choice in footwear. Other sections led us on narrow paths through wooded areas giving us a taste of Spain. From out of nowhere, a stampede of big Brown Swiss cows claimed the trail as their own, and we let them. It was like the running of the bulls. We were grateful to get a short reprieve from dodging horned animals and riding the sandy waves when the path opened up and flattened some.

Quite a while into our trek, I realized the sun was not going to stay out forever and was, in fact, getting ready for bed. Getting lost in the dark on a mountain in Haiti was probably not a good look for the director of an organization, the leader of a team of med students. *Dark* means dark, no street lights, no house lights, no houses for house lights, no light at all.

I pulled out my cell phone with the tiny battery icon showing red, hoping for some signal that until then had been absent. Excited to see a bar, I wanted to get in touch with Gardy or, better yet, Bruns, who made the trip with us from Port au Prince to translate and bodyguard.

I knew that everyone must be worried sick. The walkers would discover we didn't ride and the riders that we didn't walk—with the group anyway. For all they knew, the next time they would see us would be on the side of a milk carton. Finding us on a gigantic mountain soon to be covered with an ominous black blanket would be impossible. They had to be frantic, calling the embassy, UN police, maybe even the president, demanding that someone launch a helicopter rescue. Having both your leader and classmate missing in action was certainly causing great distress. I was sick picturing what everyone was going through. I had to let them know we were safe and not to panic. Get a helicopter, but don't panic.

Since I didn't have Brun's number and remembered that Gardy's cell phone lost its charge hours ago, I called Father Roosevelt, who is on other mountains on the other side of the capital but would hopefully be able to get in touch with someone.

The weak signal barely made a connection.

"Father, it's Kim."

"Oh, hello, Kim, I was going to call you today. I have a project. I need some help."

"Later, Father. I am on a mountain."

"Yes, I am on a mountain."

"No, Father, I am on a mountain by Rousseau."

"No, Kim. I am not in Rousseau, I'm in Morne l'hopital."

"No, I am in Rouss . . . do you have Brun's number?"

"I don't think so, but I can see."

Fearing that I was going to lose the charge at any moment, I changed my ask. "Could you please call Patrick and tell him to call Brun and tell Brun to find Gardy and just say, 'Dahlia and Kim are OK'?"

Like that would ever work. The telephone game in Haiti is just like at any ten-year-old girls' slumber party. By the end of the phone calls, someone will think "the doll with Tim found a snake."

What have I gotten myself and, more importantly, Dahlia, into? It was getting darker by the second, no shelter in sight, but oh, what a beautiful view. Still way up the mountain, it was breathtaking looking over the landscape to the sea down below. I thought about throwing my arms out and running in a circle singing, "The Sound of Music," but there was no time, and I can't sing. So, instead, I threw my arms up and said, "Lord Jesus, a little help here, please."

Jesus said, "I got ya," then from literally out of nowhere, two men and a woman appeared. Human life, so beautiful to see.

"Rousseau la?"

"Wi." Yes!

I thought I'd push a little further. "OSAPO?"

"Wi."

Even more. "Dr. Gardy?"

"Wi!" Wi indeed, as in they know not just the town and the clinic but the man himself. Wi as in we might find home before dawn.

When one of the men used the same full hand "follow me" signal that the giggling girls did a few hours ago, love trusts, so follow we did.

We made up a lot of ground quickly, having the men help us slide down the steep declines of shifting sand, then walk beside us over rocky areas to make sure we didn't fall or, more accurately, catch us when we did. Darkness took over the mountain, and the trio was unfazed. Marching on, marching down, marching closer to home with each step.

Because it was as black as shoe polish, neither Dahlia nor I saw that we had landed on a road. One last step off the bluff and we were standing on flat, solid ground.

"Mesi! Mesi!" We hugged our navigators. "Dahlia, we made it." I didn't want to sound surprised—relieved maybe, but surprise would indicate a lack of trust and love doesn't lack that.

A handful of people were gathered in front of a structure the size of an outhouse buying beverages. I had no money, but seconds later, there was a cold bottle of water in my hand. These people sure know how to love. Then we stood there, then stood there some more. I wondered if they thought we would know the way from this spot, but I had no idea where we were. Then I heard it, the beautiful melody of a moto. We were waiting for a ride. That is why they had us stand there. Nice. Just trust, because love trusts.

The first moto that scooted by had four people aboard, so no room for us. Several minutes later, another passed, again loaded beyond capacity. Finally, a motorcycle taxi pulled up beautifully unoccupied. I had Dahlia straddle the seat right behind the driver, so if anyone fell off, it would be me. I hugged and thanked our new friends. I had nothing to give them, no money, no anything. I wanted so badly to do something for them even though nothing was expected because they understand no-expectations, kind love. I looked down so as not to stumble on rocks and saw bare feet. I had forgotten that the female part of our trailblazing crew broke her sandals right at the end of our journey. I quickly took mine off, handed them to her, hugged her again, and hopped on behind Dahlia. Then, as if they hadn't done enough for us already, one of the gentlemen hopped on behind me. I would not fall off after all.

Pulling up to OSAPO, I felt a small inkling of what it must be like to be a soldier returning from the war, heading down the tarmac to be greeted by family and with balloons, flowers, and banners. But there were no balloons, flowers, banners. Or family and friends!

A few from our group were mingling outside buying last-minute handicrafts from a couple of local ladies.

"We're here!"

"Yep, hey, what should I pay for the turtle?" Korrine was in the middle of negotiations.

"Weren't you worried?"

"About what?"

"That we were missing."

"Missing? Nobody said anything."

All my worry about their worry and all along there was no worry. They were not even aware that we were missing, too busy packing and purchasing to notice. They didn't count because that was my job. They just trusted. Because that is what love does.

Trusting Love

Trusting love appreciates the fact that you don't have to know everything or have all of the answers. You can trust that someone knows something that you don't. When you love, you know that you don't know it all. So love that always trusts reaches out and asks for answers. It recognizes that those you love have knowledge beyond yours. It realizes that we do so much better, live so much happier, love so much deeper when we do it together. And together, we know a whole lot more than any one individual.

Love that always trusts is humble, not an arrogant know-it-all, discrediting others' experience and knowledge. It doesn't assume deceit but rather assumes truth and takes people at their word. I am not talking about things that people read and relay and might have misunderstood or didn't quite get the statistic exactly right. Those are just honest mistakes—not lying, just retelling as they remember it. I am referring to loving people so much that you value their opinion, knowledge, and wisdom because love always trusts. You can ask for advice because love always trusts. You can let your guard down, ask for help, and break away from cynicism because love always trusts.

At first this seemed naive in some ways. But I found that believing people, trusting their truthfulness, changes things. Before learning this, I would be cautious, suspicious even, trying to sort truth from fiction. Once I started living love that always trusts, conversations changed. In fact, conversations not only changed, they happened. Communicating with someone when you are not constantly looking for lies is marvelous. When you realize that their beliefs and opinions are just as valid to them as your beliefs and opinions are to you, confrontations become conversations. Conversations help reveal truth. By living trusting love in listening, it is amazing what you can learn.

What I found is that living love that always trusts brings out the best in people. Being trusted makes you want to be worthy of that trust. We all want to be trusted. Mistrust can eat at your soul. Trust someone with a key to your house and they become your home security system. Trust someone to take care of your pooch when you go away to the tropics and you will come home to a happy, well-groomed dog. Trust someone with extra duties at work, a new project to complete, a meeting to plan, and it is surprising how people come through and quite often go above and beyond because you trusted them.

When my kids were in early elementary school, the questions during dinner were always the same. "Did you have a nice day?" "Did you learn anything?" "Did you do your homework?" After a few years, the dialogue changed, and the "Did you do your homework" question left the conversation. We trusted our kids to get their homework done. We expected good grades, and good grades come with turning in your homework, so the question wasn't necessary. By trusting, they learned it was on them, so they did it.

Love that always trusts, trusts that someone's got your back, you are not alone. It can be so easy to jump ahead when an answer isn't coming at the right time on your gotta-have-an-answer-now watch. But God knows everything, God cares wholly, God loves unfailingly, and love always trusts.

Lord Jesus, help me to trust with love that trusts. Help me to be trustworthy. Help me to take people at their word, loving them enough to trust them.

CHAPTER 13

LOVE ALWAYS HOPES

Hope, what would we do without you? In the middle of the floods, you are our boat. When everything looks bleak, you are our squeegee. When we are exhausted from life's heaviness, you are our snow day. For sure, love always hopes. This might be the easiest one yet. I almost feel like I could stop typing right here and just say, "Yes, it does."

But I am sure that there is more. Because with God, love is enormous, multifaceted, complex yet simple, overflowing fullness, but there is always room for more.

I have hoped. I have hope. Some things that I hoped for came to fruition. Other hopes have been pulverized, chewed up, and spit out.

One thing that I hoped for was some help. I had four kids at home, a full-time job, a varsity volleyball coaching position, leadership duties at church, a gym membership, a van that required a hazmat suit to enter, and a laundry pile that made Mount Everest jealous. There was so little time for dusting that Noah started naming the bunnies. Vacuuming? I think I remember doing that sometimes. The kids did the dishes. Little did they know they could have asked for a whole lot more allowance to ease that never-ending burden. I scrubbed showers when I scrubbed myself. Fortunately, toilets basically clean themselves every time they flush. Oh boy, I hoped for help.

The conversation with Steve went something like this.

"Please, you have to do something."

"I do stuff."

"When your jobs are taking out the trash and mowing the lawn, you aren't exactly overloaded in Michigan in January."

"I do dishes."

"Emptying the dishwasher once a month doesn't exactly equate to doing the dishes."

"What then?"

"You pick, laundry or dinner every night." I would scrub an entire gym floor with a toothbrush if it meant not having to do laundry or make dinner. Laundry grows. I cannot explain it, but I would finish folding the last load of anything cloth and dirty in the house, walk upstairs to put away the very last towels, and by the time I walked back down, the laundry room floor would be full again, like some vicious joke, or a nightmare that has you trapped in a maze of mirrors. Laundry grows, and socks disappear. Poof. Here today, gone tomorrow. The only time any of us wore a matching pair of socks was when they came out of the package on Christmas morning. Our extended family found it amusing—extended family without sock eaters.

And dinner. Every single night these kids wanted to eat. Every. Single. Night. Breakfast and lunch were easy. A box of cereal, a gallon of milk, a loaf of Wonder Bread, and a jar of peanut butter. Simple. On the other hand, dinner required things like noodles, raw chicken, potatoes, and frozen vegetables. First, you had to go get all of those things, then bring them into the house, put them somewhere, find them again, and try to mix them into something that could pass as a meal. Don't let those one-pan recipe books fool you. You need a pan to make a sauce, and another pan to brown the hamburger, and then put it all in a third pan to cook it. I tried getting away with spaghetti every night: some ground beef, a jar of Prego, noodles, and voila, protein, vegetables, and a starch, a complete meal. Those kids caught on pretty fast. They wanted variety and made it known that switching between spaghetti, fettuccine, and egg noodles didn't constitute variety.

After I spent hours and hours and hours in the kitchen, today my kids can't even remember me cooking. I should have just kept rotating noodles. They wouldn't remember.

So, I put it out there. Two of the most painful jobs known to mankind, right up there with pet food taster, roadkill collector, and manual sewer cleaner. Pick one and I promise to embrace the other.

"I'll take laundry."

Whew, way easier than I thought. Great news. I might just use a clean towel after I shower tonight to celebrate.

Busy days went by. I had dinner on the table every night; laundry was dead to me. I felt so free, so light, having so much extra time on my hands. I even thought about dusting, which was a lot farther than I had gone down that road in a while.

After a week or so, I noticed that I was down to one clean pair of underwear. I had one more day before I had to start wearing them inside out. Victoria's Secret bailed me out, and I had a whole week's worth of new silky drawers. Seven days later, I shopped again. Then again. I told Steve that not doing the laundry was getting pretty expensive, so he went to work.

The first thing he did was throw away every sock in the house. Athletic socks, ankle socks, dress socks, knee highs, all went in the garbage that he took to the curb, because that was his job.

Then Steve went to Sam's Club. He bought twelve packages of twelve pairs of white calf-high athletic socks. He thought he was a genius. His friends high-fived him. Men approached him at the grocery store, wanting to shake the hand of the legend. He started signing autographs. He was a sock rock star.

Except the socks were identical and they all fit the size-thirteen feet of my six-foot-three husband. The heel of the sock landed about mid calf for me. But I was not going to complain. I was still basking in the laundry-free sun.

Before too long, some of those bright white socks turned pink.

College failed him with no class about avoiding anything red in a load of everything else white. Still, I let it go. It was no longer my job. I had a great underwear wardrobe, a big job off my shoulders, and I like pink.

One Saturday morning, I saw a very unfamiliar sight. One of my sons was carrying a laundry basket.

"What are you doing?"

"Duh. Laundry."

That pink-sock maker taught the kids how to do their own laundry. I was sweating over a hot stove, poring over recipes, and making multiple trips to the grocery store, while my offspring were washing, drying, folding, and putting away.

I hoped for help. I got it. I was expecting two hands and ended up with ten. Hope doesn't always look the way we expect.

Uplifting Hope

I hope for things all the time. I hope it doesn't rain when I go to the beach. I hope I don't get a flat tire. I hope my condo fees don't increase. I hope the plane is on time, the restaurant has a table available, and that I don't have any cavities. I don't have just personal hopes, I hope for others too. I hope she lands that job, they find a house, his athlete's foot disappears. I hope Harrison sinks that shot, Cordelia makes the team, and Rosemary never loses her spunk. More profound hopes: I hope their marriage stays together, her mother fully recovers, and his diabetes remains under control.

Some hopes are unrealistic. Steve was a pessimist, and I am an optimist. He'd say he was a realist and I lived in la-la land. I'd rather be a daydream believer walking on sunshine somewhere over the rainbow than be the same old song sitting under a blue moon crying the tears of a clown. My hopes and life's reality don't always hang out together on the same corner. I hope I win the Mega Millions jackpot. I hope my car can make it all the way home on fumes. I hope dinner tastes better than it looks. Some of my la-la hopes I won't give up. I hope for world peace. I hope for social justice. I hope for an end to poverty.

Everybody hopes. Some the same and some completely different. Some personal, some outward.

Hope is uplifting, rejuvenating, inspiring. Hope anticipates, expects, believes. Hope sees possibilities and seeks opportunities. Hope is a yearning, a dream, a belief in something more, better, higher. Love that always hopes has to be something special beyond "I hope you have a great day."

Hope in Haiti? What else is there? Hope for food today, hope for a little money to buy it, hope for a place to live, hope for a school for your kids, and hope for a little electricity at night. With most things so unpredictable, hope is all you've got; fortunately, with God that's a lot. I have high hopes, high apple-pie-in-the-sky hopes, that I can figure this one out.

A team of medical students and doctors from Wayne State University joined me in Morne l'hopital, a densely populated mountain community overlooking Port au Prince. Small concrete block structures stacked like stair steps house nearly 250,000 people with no latrines, no potable water, and almost no medical care. The area has been heavily deforested, allowing even short rains to bring big floods. Transportation is an issue. The roads are often undrivable due to the rivers of water creating trenches much larger than Michigan's biggest potholes. Tap taps and taxis do not make the trip up the mountain. The jobs are in Port au Prince, and Morne l'hopital residents fortunate enough to have one walk miles uphill after a day of hard work. With jobs as scarce as trees, families live on less than $150 a year. Anyone in need of medical care has very few options. Anyone in need of emergency medical care is almost hopeless.

For several years, Wayne State University medical students and doctors partnered with Rays of Hope to set up weeklong medical clinics in December, February, and sometimes May. HART, Haiti and Africa Relief Team, also holds clinics annually, making medical care available just three to four times a year.

Father Roosevelt hosts the groups in his rectory across the dirt road from St. Jude's Catholic Church and School, a big main room surrounded on three sides by six bedrooms and three bathrooms, leaving the fourth side for the kitchen.

Meals at Father's never disappoint. The cooks combine Haitian spaghetti, noodles tossed in a frying pan with tomato paste or ketchup, garlic, onion, peppers, and sometimes hotdogs for a breakfast favorite with a hint of heat. Bread straight out of the stone oven up the street with peanut butter and jelly filled the void until dinner, when the cooks put chicken, potatoes, rice, beans, spices, and vegetables together in ways my kids only dreamed of. Great skills, delicious food, beautiful hearts—the ladies know how to keep us coming back.

The medical team used the church as a triage and waiting room, and six small rooms down a short hill served as exam spaces and pharmacy.

Lynda, Rays of Hope's Queen Lynda, registered nurse and master of all things medical, worked in an emergency room in Muskegon, Michigan, for more than twenty-five years. She thought she had seen it all until her first visit to Haiti. With patient sheets, a pen, and Patrick to translate, Lynda would triage the near thousand people who came through the gate desperate to see a doctor. With her bag of Dum Dums, she asked questions, wrote notes, prioritized. She dispensed one nasty tasting, chewable Vermox for worms, followed quickly by a sucker chaser.

Every morning, the group weaved through a maze of mommas holding babies, dads with small children draped over their arms, elderly women being supported by sticks acting as canes, young children guarding a younger sibling, old men with weathered faces, all hoping to be one of those lucky to meet Lynda. Love hopes, always.

Once Lynda was ready, hired police officers acting as gatekeepers called out numbers and escorted patients to the waiting area. Medical students took turns taking vitals and histories. Having made frequent visits to Haiti, Lynda knew a lot of them by name and nearly all of them by sight and ailment. She listened, dewormed, and suckered, then sent them down to see a doctor.

"Look, it's the guy with the foot."

Lynda was excited to see a man she met the year before who was carried to the clinic with the worst case of gangrene anyone had ever seen. Nobody thought he would live to see the next month, certainly not the next year. Lynda hoped he would defy death because love always hopes, and Lynda loves. Looking so much more alive, he gave her a hug before he took off his boot. This time there was no room-clearing odor; he had followed directions, cleaned regularly, and had his disease under control.

A father carried in his epileptic fourteen-year-old son, begging for help. Lynda knew this man too. Seizures quite often require medicine to control. Seizure medicine like phenobarbital, so plentiful and inexpensive in the United States, seldom make it to the shores of Haiti. This boy's dad carried his boy, nearly a man now, several miles every time doctors were at Father's. This time like the times before we arranged for Patrick to take the pair to a clinic in Port au Prince, the only clinic we were aware of that treated, or tried to treat, epilepsy. As we gave Patrick the twenty-dollar entrance fee, the man hoped that this time would be different, this time his son would be given something to stop his seizures, seizures that had wreaked havoc on the boy's body and, more sadly, his brain. I cried. I remember well those awful days with my daughter and son who had EEGs, CAT scans, MRIs, medicine, and regular visits to a neurologist. My daughter and son, living in the United States, received medical care that prevented their brains from suffering the effects of unmanaged seizures. Lynda and I hoped and prayed.

Always many visited with expected ailments due to dehydration, contaminated drinking water, and malnourishment. Hypertension led to blood pressures high enough to send people to the hospital in the States, but in Haiti it just sent them home on medicine, medicine that we tried to make sure could be refilled in Haiti. Vitamin deficiencies, cholera, a rare case of malaria, broken bones that had healed poorly without a cast or splint, infected wounds that are difficult to keep clean when dirt is the flooring in your house, scabies, heart issues.

Other patients had cultural illnesses. When Lynda looked baffled by a patient's story, Patrick always said, "It's a Haitian thing." Like the woman who said she had been pregnant for four years or the woman with a swollen belly who was sure whatever was moving inside was not a baby because she only had done it in the ocean where you can't conceive.

During a weeklong Wayne State medical clinic in Haiti, a man came in actively having a heart attack. I grabbed a driver; Dr. Laura helped the man into the SUV and then hopped in beside him. I rode shotgun, telling the driver to go faster and faster. Arriving safely at the nearest hospital, our driver helped Dr. Laura and me get him inside, where we were told to take a number and a seat. Dr. Laura was hot. She asked to see a cardiologist, ER doc, anyone, but the woman behind the desk just shook her head. The driver stayed with the man while the two of us went running down the halls calling for help. Finally, a doctor answered and came to see the man in the waiting room. It was probably twenty minutes but seemed like much more before a wheel-chair moved him to a large ward with thirty or more beds. The staff took immediate control and did everything they could for our guy. Seeing the gunshot wounds of the man on his right and head injury of the man on his left, it was clear to us why a heart attack didn't receive immediate attention. Everyone in the ward, from babies to adults, had severe, life-threatening injuries or illnesses. A heart attack was just one more for the skeleton crew. Dr. Laura and I left, hoping the man would be all right.

We set up by 8 a.m. and worked as many hours as possible. Knowing we had virtually no light after sunset, we pushed the limits and saw the last few patients of each day under flashlights.

Dinner gave new energy to the crew after such long, exhausting days. Each night we played games like Heads Up, Celebrity, and Scissor Bag, a game that took years of yoga, flexibility training, and incredible ninja skills.

As I walked back and forth between the rectory and the church every day, people would beg, plead with me to bring them in. After running many clinics for many years, I figure I have an honorary med-ical degree of some kind and would often bring someone through the gate past the guards. The others always understood because they too could see the urgency for one of their neighbors. Lynda would roll her eyes and say, "What do you have now?" I would give her my impassioned spiel about the poor lethargic baby who has not eaten in a couple of days or the man who thinks he is losing his arm. Sometimes my instincts were right; other times, she sent the patient to the back of the line, but always she let them stay and be seen.

Identifying with Others' Hope

The last day brought mixed emotions. Tired, ready for home, seeing the end in sight felt great. But seeing the scads of people that time would not allow to be seen broke our hearts, made us feel lousy.

That morning, knowing that the number of people already in the church would take us until well after dark to treat, I made my way through the crowd saying, *"Mwen regrèt. Mwen regrèt."* I'm sorry. I'm sorry. A man and woman caught my attention. Their eyes teeming with desperation, the man took my hand and put it on his wife's breast, where a large mass was evident. A few years back, I had a mass. Positive that it was nothing, I fought getting a mammogram. With no history of breast cancer in my family, in my mid forties, and healthy, I saw it as a way for the medical world to make some money.

Going to the Betty Ford clinic kicking and screaming, I told the sweet ladies that I understood it was their job to talk to me about lumps and self-exams and regular mammograms, but I was only there to appease my doctor. Just wanted to get in, have the waffle iron compress my tata into batter-based breakfast food, and send me on my jolly way.

They told me like every other woman in the pink, tie-in-the-front half robes that they would let me know when I was "free to go." Impatiently tapping my fingers on the table next to my chair, I heard everyone getting a "See you next year!" and I was anxious for mine. Instead, I got a "Kim, will you follow me, please?" Was that a yes or no question? Follow you where? Maybe the test didn't take, and I have to go through that fiendish torture again. A man must have created that machine.

When we went back into the little room, the very kind lady in white told me not to worry, but the doctor would like to do an ultrasound. The ultrasound led to an appointment for a biopsy. Still 100 percent certain I was wasting my time, I was a good little doobie, and let them stick me with a big needle as my breasts dangled down through the hole in the table they had me lie on. On my birthday, no less. "This won't hurt." Yeah, right.

Two days later, a Friday afternoon at about 3 p.m., I was watching a couple of my grandbabies play in the tub when my phone rang. "Kim, the results are in. You have breast cancer, blah, blah, blah. We will call you on Tuesday to make an appointment. Blah, blah, blah."

My mind went numb. I yelled for my son to watch the babies, then called Steve at work. My chest was heaving, tears were streaming, and I couldn't catch my breath.

"What's wrong! What's going on?"

"I . . . have . . . breast cancer."

Time melted like a snowball. It felt like before I had another thought, Steve was holding me tightly in his arms. It was the perfect thing to do. Somehow the man who didn't know the socks would turn pink knew exactly what to do now at the exact right moment. We stood there for a long time, crying together. Then prayed. Then hoped. Because love always does.

A month and a half later, I had a bilateral mastectomy, followed by weeks of appointments with fluid being pumped into expanders, a little break for Christmas, then because of hormone receptors, a total hysterectomy and one week later a new diagnosis. This time not mine, but Steve's. Hearing "cancer" again just four months after the first time was mind-blowing. Hearing "pancreatic cancer" was absolutely devastating. This time I held him, but I was the only one crying. "Don't cry for me. God is good."

We never lost hope, but hope changed. We prayed, "Lord Jesus, please either bring healing like you did to the blind and the lame or give him the ultimate healing, heaven. But please, don't let him suffer."

God really is good. All the time. We had a great time together at home. Side by side, watching Cash Cab and Sports Center, playing cards, and playing with the grandbabies. Got unimaginable support from our kids, other family, and friends. And when Steve woke up in pain on that Sunday morning just six weeks after his diagnosis, I held him as tight as I could and whispered in his ear, "You can go."

Standing on that dirt road in Haiti brought back all of the emotion, the memories, and the pain.

I brought Ramone and Vesta with five-month-old David in her arms to Lynda, who sent us down to Dr. Diane Levine, the absolute picture of an amazing doctor whose abundant talent was only outshined by her compassion.

Vesta was four months pregnant when she discovered the lump. Afraid to say anything about it, she decided to wait until after the baby was born to tell Ramone and seek advice. Vesta and Ramone met when they were only ten years old and were friends for a long time before becoming more when they were fourteen. They married at eighteen and more in love than ever. Babies started coming. Ramone worked hard to support the family, and he did. They had a roof over their heads and food on the table. Vesta started a vending business selling crackers, cookies, and chips to help make ends meet. So distraught about this lump, which had grown significantly since she found it, now the size of an orange, she hadn't picked the vending business back up since giving birth to baby number five.

I stayed with her, holding her hand, as Dr. Levine used the portable ultrasound machine the team brought with them. Dr. Levine was as certain as she could be without a biopsy that the tumor was cancerous. We all cried together for a couple of minutes. What was this poor man going to do if something happened to the love of his life and mother of his children?

Then hope came busting through the door.

"Vesta, don't lose hope. I went through it and here I am."

I showed her my scars, talked to her about surgery, and told her that there was a ton of hope, that I know an oncologist from the States working in Haiti and would contact him immediately. We would pray and hope and pray some more. We sat together, the five of us, Dr. Levine answering every question while Ramone held on to Vesta from behind, David sleeping peacefully in my arms. We stayed together for a couple of hours. I called my oncologist friend. At his recommendation, I arranged for a drive to take Vesta, Ramone, and breastfeeding David to Mirebalais, where Partners in Health built a brand-new hospital. It just so happened that they would be holding an open clinic the next day, so all Vesta had to do was show up. I gave them money for food and more. I paid the driver. I looked Vesta in the eyes and said, "You may not lose hope. I am not going to lose hope for you. I am going to dance with you at David's wedding." She smiled and said, "I love you." I said, "I love you too." Because love always hopes.

Love that always hopes never gives up on anyone. Never quits, never stops, never gives in. Love never stops hoping that there will be recovery from the addiction, healing from the sickness, restoration of a relationship. Love that always hopes loves in such a way that you see the future as brighter, something really good coming out of something crummy, and miracles before they happen. Love that always hopes, hopes for good, happiness, and joy for everyone because you love them all. Even those who have hurt you; love always hopes for the best for them too. Love that always hopes does not mean that you have to stay in an abusive relationship or an ugly friendship. Love that always hopes, hopes good stuff for the husband, wife, friend, cousin, neighbor, sister, brother. Love that always hopes always loves, because when you love it changes your heart. And when you love it can change their heart too. Because there is always hope when there is love. Because hope is what love does.

Going back to Haiti a few months later, I got to hold a much bigger David again. Vesta, Ramone, and David made the two-hour drive to Mirebalais but didn't see a doctor. I have no idea why. They waited, and at the end of the day, they made the two-hour drive back. They never gave up hope. As strong as their bond was before, God poured on some Gorilla Glue and connected their souls even tighter. They prayed, hoped, believed, never gave up, never gave in, never stopped.

Surrounded by the peace that surpasses understanding, clothed in hope and love, Vesta took my hand and placed it on her breast. The tumor was almost completely gone. Because God loves, he doesn't lose hope either or give up on us. Thank you for that!

> *Lord Jesus, I pray that I love that way. Never giving up. How often have I wanted to throw in the towel on someone, raise the white flag, give in? Never again. Because love always hopes. Help me to see when I am not loving that way. Help me to love with a love that always hopes because my hope is in you.*

CHAPTER 14

LOVE ALWAYS PERSEVERES

PERSEVERE: A VERB, AN ACTION, "to maintain a purpose despite difficulty, obstacles, or discouragement," says dictionary.com. No quitting, no whining, just do it.

Love always perseveres. It must love relentlessly, through hard times or situations, pushing through it all.

The same website says to persevere is to bolster, sustain, and uphold. All walk and not just talk. Living love.

In a story Jesus told, a widow persistently kept badgering and badgering a judge. Her rights violated, she pleaded fervently for justice and protection. The widow would not stop until he acted. Day after day, she harassed him, begging for him to listen. Even though he ignored her pleas for quite a while, she refused to give up. The judge had no love for God, her, or anyone else; nevertheless, she wore him out. He just couldn't take it anymore. Knowing the only way to get peace was to rule in her favor, he did.

It makes sense, Jesus says, that love changes the story. This judge sought justice despite his apathy. How much more does God, who cares and loves, listen to our petitions? Show steadfast perseverance, never wave a white flag, pray without ceasing, and know that God will bring speedy justice. Then Jesus wonders aloud if he will find this level of tenacity when he comes again. Fascinating.

Love always perseveres. We can't stop. No matter how hard.

There is a reason Paul threw this word in at the end. I just need to find out why.

Being a widow, I find it interesting that the story giving us instructions to persevere, not give up, is about a woman like me.

Persevering Need

About a year after losing Steve, I called my megachurch to find out what they offered for women in my situation. One of the pastors on staff called back and set up a time to meet for coffee. I thought I was just looking for a list of potlucks, bus trips, and bingo nights.

Widowed in my forties, I assumed most of the ladies would be members of the Red Hat Society, women with more years of wisdom I could glean. But I like coffee, and the opportunities must be far too many to give over the phone. So, a couple days later, there we were, across a small table from each other marveling at the beautiful designs created in our Madcap cappuccino foam.

"So, you want to know what the church offers for widows."

"Yep."

"Absolutely nothing."

"Really?" A church with six thousand members offers nothing for widows? That was a short list; you could have told me that over the phone. Maybe they just needed a volunteer. "I'd be happy to get something going."

"Oh no, no way, we will never allow that."

"Huh?"

"We had a singles group before, and all people did was hook up."

What's wrong with people hooking up at church? Is hooking up bad? Maybe it doesn't mean the same thing as it did thirty years ago when I was trying to hook someone. Besides, I said widows, not widows and widowers. I don't think you have to worry about a room full of bereaved women "hooking up."

"Why wouldn't you want people to meet at church?"

"We will never allow anything like that again. It was a bad situation."

Was the coffee bad? Someone got upset with their table tennis partner? What atrocities accounted for this level of trepidation?

"So, where are people supposed to meet? The bars?" Certainly not the bars, right?

"No, of course not."

Whew, I'm glad he doesn't think I should "hook up" at a bar. "Then, where?"

"Well, where did you meet your husband?"

"My friend was dating his brother. Where did you meet your wife?"

An angelic glow surrounded him as he gazed up at the ceiling, imagining the moment all over again. "I will never forget that day. I was in the cafeteria at Wheaton College and glanced up to see this vision of beauty coming down the stairs. I couldn't take my eyes off of her. I knew right then and there that she would be my wife."

Nice. I kind of like to know a bit about a person, name, maybe a couple of likes and dislikes, any allergies, chronic foot odor, something, before committing to "till death do you part." But, hey, different strokes for different folks.

"OK, so?"

"So, there you go. You met your husband through a friend; I met my wife at school. That's how people meet people."

"All of my friends are married, and I don't plan on going back to school. If I did, I don't think my kids would be happy if they had to start calling one of their peers Daddy."

"Well, your choice." My choice? That is my choice? Don't meet at church, no way. You might settle for a nice Christian man when you could have landed an unbelieving, undedicated, aimless dude who didn't treat you the way you deserve. What kind of choice is that?

Buddy, stay in your lane. I didn't come here for dating advice. "I was actually talking about something for widows; widows are all women. Like a support group of some kind."

"We have groups. There are a ton of small groups at church. Just join one of those."

This guy is dense. "Do you have friends?"

"Sure! Plenty."

"Do you golf with your friends?"

"I'm on the men's league at church."

"Is it all golfers, or are there some water polo players in the mix?"

"What?"

"I'm just curious. Do all the guys use golf clubs or do some show up with baseball bats and hockey sticks?"

"Funny! Can you imagine?"

"No. I can't. Just like I can't imagine going to a small group full of couples for widow support."

"Huh? What would you even do in a [air quotes] widows' club?" The answer is yes, he is dense.

Breathe. New approach. "Are there a lot of people who want an opportunity to volunteer at church?"

"Always."

"What if there was a list of men with skills like mechanics, water heater guys, handymen, so if a widow has an issue, one of those guys could help out? Women notoriously get taken advantage of getting their car or furnace fixed. It would be nice to have someone trustworthy take a look."

"You expect them to work for you for free?"

Who hired this guy? "I think there are men who would volunteer to see if they could fix something at a reasonable price before widows in the church are overpaying some unknown company to check it out."

"That would never work." Is there anything that would ever work for you? "You want a married man to go to a single woman's house to fix things. Can you imagine what the wives would think?"

"Just so you know, being a widow does not make you hot to trot.

Besides, it would be great for the wife to be there too. The ladies could talk over a cup of coffee."

"No, no, no." Looking down as if in disgust, shaking his head, giving me not one but three nos. What is it with this guy? Is he representing the whole church leadership? Does the church leadership have any idea who they picked to tango with me?

"No, absolutely not, never, ever, no way, no how, not going to happen." I thought he was pretty clear after the first no, no, no. Maybe he thought I was the dense one.

"Isn't it the church's duty to take care of widows?"

"Um, no."

"No? We are a people group in the Bible. Lots of verses talk about taking care of widows." Read James 1:27 much? Religion that is pure and holy is to take care of widows and orphans, also known as the fatherless, in their time of need. *I hope you didn't have to pay too much for Bible college.*

"That doesn't mean now." Scoff. "That was for back then."

"Huh?" My scoff was not nearly as good as his.

"Back then, a woman was taking care of the children and the house. If her husband died, she didn't have any way to feed her family."

"Kind of like how now when a woman puts her career, schooling even, on hold to stay home to take care of the children? When her husband, who was making eighty thousand dollars a year, dies and she has been out of the job market for fifteen years, what is she supposed to do?"

"Well, there are plenty of waitress jobs around." Waitress jobs? Just a tad sexist, with a side of arrogance seasoned with ignorance.

"OK, she gets a waitress job. Working what, nights? Making how much? Maybe twenty thousand dollars a year?"

"Oh, probably not that much." Buddy, you are digging a deeper hole. Put the shovel away.

"So her kids, who just lost their dad, not only have to spend their evenings with a babysitter, that somehow less than twenty thousand dollars a year has to pay for, rather than spending the evening with their one remaining parent, but now they have to move out of their house because her measly waitress job is not going to pay the mortgage and taxes on the house near their school in the suburbs."

"Probably." Oh my gosh. Am I speaking a different language? Where is the translator? Or does the church not allow a translator around a frisky wench like me?

"Just so I'm clear. A widow not being able to support her family then is different than a widow not being able to support her family now how?"

"Stuff happens. So she has to get a job and move. What do you think? That the church should support her?" Like I'm the idiot. How foolish of me to think that a "church" practicing "religion" should help poor Jezebel the waitress.

"But we're a people group!" What next? Are you going to tell me that women, especially widows, have to be quiet in church, subservient at all times, and keep their opinions to themselves?

He laughed. He laughed! How dare he. Why doesn't he just hand me a rag so I can polish his shoes?

"We are! *Widow* appears eighty-one times in the Bible." And 80 percent of widows leave their church. Now I see why.

"I don't know what to tell you. I have a degree in theology. I have been a pastor for eighteen years. Trust me. It's not our job." Trust you? Like love trusts? Shoot! Where has love been in this whole conversation? I am not feeling it; I'm also not giving it. I persisted, I persevered, even though it was difficult. He threw out obstacles and tried his best to discourage me. But I hung in, kept fighting, and still didn't give up.

I stood, gave a slight nod, and said, "I believe my work here is done."

"What? Are you mad?" No, I just heard the school bell and want to look for a date.

"No, it's your church, do what you want."

Since I am a widow, I joined the statistic and changed churches. Other fun widow statistics are we lose 80 percent of our friends (the whole fifth-wheel thing), our life expectancy goes down, and we gain fifteen pounds.

I may have changed churches, but I am determined to break the other odds.

Persevering Determination

Several years ago, I met a spirited young man named Harold during a trip to Borel, a rural town north of Port au Prince. Harold's brother, Jonah, runs a school for kindergarten through eighth grade in an area with minimal education opportunities. My team stayed at a guesthouse down the road a bit, worked with the kids, helped with some projects in the area, and got a great feel for life in Haiti.

In the 1950s, the Export Import Bank of the United States, the official export credit agency for the US federal government, funded the building of a dam on the Artibonite River. Designed by the Army Corps of Engineers, the dam promised electricity for the whole country. With a reliable energy source, increased economic growth would bring more employment opportunities, better opportunities with better pay, lessening the gap between the wealthy and the poor. The second promise, that the dam would rehabilitate the land for agriculture through controlled floods, assured increased crop yields, especially rice for export.

Fifteen years after the dam was completed, the Péligre Hydroelectric Plant, the power plant harvesting the hydroelectric power from the dam, opened in 1971. The plant is under the control of the Haitian government. Just 30 percent of the nation's electricity comes from the plant. What was supposed to be a savior to farmers and an answer to the country's energy shortage failed on both accounts. The electricity is mainly distributed to foreign-owned factories and homes of the wealthy in Port au Prince. Due to flooding caused by the dam, thousands of poor rural farmers were forced to give up their fertile land and seek employment in the cities or move to go farm on the hillsides under very difficult conditions and poor-quality soil. The adverse effects of the dam project greatly affected the town of Borel.

In Borel, dreams stay at the city entrance. Agriculture is the primary means of survival; with irrigation obstacles and poor soil conditions, survival is for the fittest. Sometimes rains come, and sometimes it is dry for days. Wells are expensive and cost money to maintain. Farming is neither easy nor very profitable. But the farmers persevere; they do not give up on their lands, crops, or families.

Everywhere we went, Harold would appear, his big eyes sparkling with ideas and dreams for something bigger and better for himself, his brother, and the kids at the school. His dreams watered by something other than a drip line, Harold saw a future. Living in survival mode, as people living in extreme poverty must do, means focusing on just today, today's meal, today's shelter, today's existence. Somehow Harold, though living just like everyone else in Borel, had a vision of the future that is too often buried by hunger and illness.

Always looking to do more, help more, love more, Harold came to me one day and said, "Hey, Kim, can I play for you?"

"Play what?"

"Drums, music."

"Sure." I didn't see a drum, but I have seen everything imaginable used as one in Haiti. Trees, tables, overturned buckets, metal cans, bumpers, desks, coconuts, you name it—with two hands and some rhythm, the world is your drum kit.

Harold lit up. We set a time for him and a friend to come to the guesthouse and play later that night.

The group was excited when Harold walked in with a bongo and friend Johnny with a guitar. The music they made was beyond anything I imagined. So talented, it was no wonder he had a dream.

From then on, visiting Haiti meant spending some time with Harold and band, and I became their "manager." They, of course, did all of the work. My job was to be their biggest fan, support, love them every way I could, and get them some exposure when possible.

Harold started going by Marco, his given name. Wee Wee, Bruno's nickname, was nixed when I suggested it might not have mass appeal. Johnny and Fresh completed the quartet.

The band had unflappable determination. Living together in the capital, they wrote songs, songs about disunity in the country, songs about life after the earthquake, songs about love, peace, and hope for a better future. Uplifting, heart wrenching, sometimes political, all of their songs spoke right from their hearts.

Knocking on doors, doing small gigs, earning money here and there, the foursome did anything and everything they could to stay together as a band that became a family. They love each other. They persevere.

When cholera was introduced to the country, many got sick with too many dying because they did not know how to prevent spreading or catching the infectious disease. Marco wrote a song about hygiene that the band took to the schools. No doubt it was effective. Kids went home singing it, parents learned it too, and likely hundreds if not thousands were saved with that little ditty.

Often the band would come and play when I brought a team down with me—always a highlight of the trip. Everyone dancing, singing, savoring a moment in Haiti, a reprieve from driving the littered streets lined with the ravages of poverty. The band exuded hope. Visiting a place like Haiti, hearing the stories, seeing the conditions, understanding the plight can be hope robbing. "Where do you even begin?" is a common question. "You begin with one" is always my answer. The band restored the hope that the landscape had sucked away.

One afternoon, the five of us decided it was time for a name. After kicking around a few ideas, knowing that peace and unity drove their message, 4 Harmony was birthed. Four of them, signing in harmony, desiring harmony for their country, the name is perfect.

Over time their stages and venues grew. It was always so fun to see them playing in a hotel bar or street fair. I believed in them, but way more importantly, they believed in themselves.

Trying to make it as a band anywhere is a long, hard road. Trying to make it as a band in Haiti is like pushing a freight train to the top of Mount Everest. With so many obstacles, closed doors, and rejections, the fortitude to go on takes a will of steel, four wills of steel in this case.

It made perfect sense that Marco, Fresh, Johnny, and Bruno would be on the cover of *Persevere Magazine*. And how much more perfect that I was able to meet up with the band while discovering love that always perseveres.

Every March, I look forward to spending a week with fabulous artists from the College for Creative Studies in Detroit, Michigan. Always the kindest, most inquisitive, open-minded people, they share a unique artistic bond that creates mutual respect and admiration. Since they desired total immersion into the Haitian culture, I loved taking them to places that most people, even Haitians, never see. That includes meeting local geniuses, exploring hidden galleries, teaching in classrooms, and learning from the greats, developing the same shared bond that unites artists universally.

It had been a while since we got together. Marco and the guys, all so busy, and now all so married, were still together, still working hard, still making music.

During breakfast, I said, "I have a big surprise."

All eyes turned my way, even the nearby staff at Wall's International Guest House, our home for part of the week.

"My band is coming to play tonight."

"You have a band?" I claim them as part of the family but cannot claim any responsibility for their successes.

"Yep, 4 Harmony." I heard gasps behind me. I turned to see three young ladies, staff at Wall's, with eyes wide open and hands covering mouths. Maybe they saw a tarantula.

Back at Wall's after another fantastic day with this group, we found dinner was waiting. Just sitting down to eat, I heard my name. There he stood, gleaming white tunic matching his gleaming white pants, cool aviator sunglasses, chestnut gladiator sandals, and dreads down over his shoulders. Marco.

The staff was buzzing. Pointing and giggling like Bruno Mars just walked in.

"Marco!"

"Kim!" Our usual greeting, like long-lost friends surprised to see each other somewhere in the world where neither one lives.

We hugged, and hugged some more, making up for lost time.

"What's going on?"

"A lot."

Then I noticed his entourage. Resembling Secret Service agents, I thought I saw one of them talking into his wrist, but, hey, he might have just had an itch.

We spent some time catching up. Sharing family pictures on our phones, reminiscing, chatting, and laughing felt good. It felt good to know that everyone was healthy with a roof over their heads and food on the table.

"Let me show you something." Marco pulled up a video.

With music playing in the background, cameras panned a massive crowd, then zoomed in on emcees resembling Mario Lopez in a beautifully tailed black suit and Brooke Burke in floor-length mint green sequined designer gown. The music stopped when Mario and Brooke began reading the teleprompters. The words coming quickly in Spanish flew over my head. I heard, "Something, something something, something, Ayiti." Haiti! I knew a word! "Something, something, something something, something, canta 4 Harmony." 4 Harmony? What?

A cameraman moved his attention to center stage. There, under the spotlight, stood Marco, white tunic and pants with amazing green, gold, red, and black artwork down one side, and dreads pulled back. Blowing into a conch shell, a national symbol for freedom used by Africans forced into slavery as a call to battle defeating the French, Marco! Instruments began playing and the camera switched to one positioned at the back of the venue, exposing a humongous stage, bigger than any hotel bar. Marco and the others were the size of ants from so far away. Lights flashing everywhere, and the next camera switch focused on twelve gorgeous scantily dressed women dancing in unison to the left of the stage. With the camera slowly rotating to the right, those under the lights were slowly revealed. Johnny! Bruno! Marco! Fresh! All in white with similar embellishments, Johnny playing guitar, the other three holding microphones. The guys filling the screen, Marco singing lead, the choreography continued with the dancers moving around the musicians. Astonished and mesmerized, tingles traveled up and down my spine. Unbelievable, like watching a dream.

When the song finished, Marco said, "Gracias Chile!"

Mr. Lopez said, "Gracias Ayiti!"

"What was that?"

"The International Music Competition." In Chile, where 4 Harmony performed for a sold-out crowd at the twenty thousand seat Quinta Veregara Amphitheater in Viña del Mar, Chile. It turns out 4 Harmony was invited to compete in the annual competition, held in different countries each year. And they took second place. Second place! These four guys had the stamina, the strength, and the spirit to bolster, sustain, and uphold each other, and the judge ruled in their favor. Love persevered.

"Marco, you are amazing."

A crowd had gathered. They must have heard the music.

Two teenage girls, acting starstruck, approached. They said something. Marco said something. They giggled and then handed him a piece of paper and a pen. He wrote something down and gave it back.

"What was that about?"

"Nothing, they just wanted an autograph."

An autograph.

Now 4 Harmony is the number one band in the country of eleven million people, the Beatles of Haiti. Everyone knows each one by name. I have a hard time remembering which Monkee is who, except Davy Jones, a tween crush. Not just in Haiti, not only one performance in Chile, 4 Harmony has traveled to several countries to perform. They cut a record and made a video with Tiano Bless, Chile's number one reggae singer. They are writing, recording, traveling, and performing. And grounded and humble. Marco is helping Jonah fund the school in Borel. Each one of them supports projects and people.

This is perseverance beyond all measure. Marco-Harold, the boy from one of the most impoverished areas in the poorest country in the western hemisphere, the boy who learned to play bongos by beating on buckets, the boy who asked if he could play for me, that boy, his love of Jesus, music, family, and friends, won the verdict. He also won the million-dollar judgment. Marco, Johnny, Fresh, and Bruno lived love that always perseveres.

Persevering Love

To persevere is one thing. Not giving up until the buzzer rings at the end of a game. Not quitting a job until it's finished. Making it through a tough time. Successful dieting takes perseverance. Saving money for a house takes perseverance. Training for a marathon, starting a company, raising kids, all take perseverance.

Most things that take perseverance have a beginning and an end. The buzzer rings, the job is done, the house is purchased, the weight is lost, the business is up and running, the marathon is over, the kids are grown.

Love that always perseveres has no end. When Jesus asks, "Will I see this same perseverance when I come back?" it gives me pause. If love always perseveres, then yes, it will be the same intensity. Because love always perseveres.

Marriages can, do, have peaks and valleys. Love that always perseveres does not quit; it upholds through difficulties. Then it continues on to the mountaintops.

I had a great, really great marriage. But there were a couple of times when one or the other of us felt like throwing in the towel. Or just me, after making lasagna with Barry Manilow on the stereo. But I persevered, we persevered, because that is what love does. It was up to us, up to me, to make things better, the best they could be.

Illness takes a lot of love that perseveres, not just for the one who ails but for all their people, family, friends.

I have a friend who is a gifted athlete, excelling in several sports. Hardworking, she gave it her all every time she stepped onto a court or field. Lots of friends, teammates, and family showed her lots of love. Her sophomore year of high school, rounding a base, she tore her ACL in one knee, an injury resulting in a long, tough recovery. Knowing that she loved to play sports more than anything, the people around her upheld her, persevered with her.

Thrilled to finally be fully recovered just in time for softball season, only one game in she tore her other ACL. Again, people rallied. But not as long. Her friends loved her, persevered with her the first go-around, but didn't have the stamina to do it again. My friend had no choice.

She went on to have countless surgeries. Her parents were her biggest supporters, her siblings persevering with her. But her friends, her teammates gave up. They quit before the end. So painful, more than the injury. Her friends were hanging out at the mall, going to movies, attending school parties, and having fun like teenagers. They were just doing it with one fewer person, a person they stopped visiting, stopped inviting. That's not love, because love always perseveres. But her friends were young and probably didn't know how much it hurt.

She married a great guy. He loves her with a love that always perseveres. Many surgeries happening after the "I dos," he has upheld her every step of the way. Because of one surgery that didn't go as expected, my friend lost her leg from the knee down. Some men might have walked away. But her husband loves her, fully.

She is amazingly strong. Together they are conquerors, warriors.

A wheelchair works as her legs most of the time. She works as an RN helping, loving others. They have two beautiful children and a beautiful life together because love always perseveres.

Love that always—always as in all the time for all time—perseveres, does not fade. It does not give up. It is Jesus personified. It knows that times can be tough, junk can get in the way, discouragement can come, but love fights through it. Then again, for the next thing and the next. Just like God never gives up on any of us, we should never give up on each other.

If someone chooses a path that you just can't go down and survive, you might have to walk away. But love still perseveres as you love and pray the best for them, relentlessly.

You see parents loving their kids with love that always perseveres. They may have kids in trouble, addictions, drugs, poor choices, but they love them through it all. Love that always perseveres does not mean love that always houses, always bails out, always funds, always enables. Love that always perseveres does not give up on loving. It never stops praying. Never stops.

Love always perseveres.

Lord Jesus, please help me to live this never-quit, always-bolster-up, love that always perseveres. Help me to see when I am not loving this way. Give me the tenacity of 4 Harmony to love.

LOVE NEVER FAILS

Love, when you break it down, roll it out, turn it over, shake it out, is alive. It is not just a feeling; it is living, breathing, walking, talking, doing.

Real love cannot stay hidden. It is something you give and something you live.

Loving, giving love, living love, real love, is liberating.

When you live love that is patient, you are free to be in the moment, not take the phone call, not worry about your next move. You are no longer held captive by the past, stopping your growth and the growth of relationships. You are not a servant to the future, keeping your mind always ahead of your body. Being concerned more with what is yet to happen renders this moment right now negligible. Not only do you lose out but there is also no love in that. How insignificant is the person or people in front of you? Does the importance of what is happening later justify lessening the value of who is before you now? Love that is patient stops, breathes, listens, and loves, giving your full focus to what is happening this moment. *The Message* says it this way: "Give your entire attention to what God is doing right now, and don't get worked up about what may or may not happen tomorrow. God will help you deal with whatever hard things come up when the time comes" (Matt. 6:34).

Living love that is kind releases you to give of yourself without keeping score. You can show kindness just because you desire to, because love is kind. It exempts you from expectations for reciprocal acts and it absolves you from performing reciprocal acts. A presumed or compulsory act of kindness is diluted. Love that is kind is authentic. Love that is kind does not do a kind act for notoriety or publicity. Love that is kind comes entirely from the heart, with no ego or hope for reward. Jesus lived love that is kind, healing the sick, caring for the poor, feeding the masses. He did not need or want anyone to know about his kind acts and, in fact, often commanded the recipients not to tell anyone. He did not desire attention or accolades. Jesus wanted all emphasis on his message, his love. Like when Jesus took the hand of a little girl who died and said, "My child, get up!" Right away, she stood, breathing again. He told her ecstatic parents not to tell anyone what happened (Luke 8:51–56). No spotlights or billboards. Just kind love.

Love does not boast. It takes away the pressure of the pedestal. The taller the pillar, the harder the fall. Your horn staying untooted, you don't have to be in the limelight, the one who is always right, the one who is the ultimate winner of intellectual debates. Love that does not boast does not elevate oneself. Love that does not boast recognizes equality: everyone parallel, everyone loved, everyone heard. "Do nothing out of selfish ambition or vain conceit. Rather, in humility value others above yourselves, not looking to your own interests but each of you to the interests of the others" (Phil. 2:3–4).

Love that is not proud is humble; it has no barricades, it lets others in. Humble love also lets others love you, acknowledging there may be more than one way to do something, more than one way to see, more than one answer. Love that is not proud grows, learns, opens its mind. Love that is not proud gives you permission to change or tweak your views, humbling yourself and knowing that something could be different from what you believe. Love that is not proud realizes you don't know it all and loves loving others enough to respect their opinions, knowledge, and wisdom. "When pride comes, then comes disgrace, but with humility comes wisdom" (Prov. 11:2).

Love that does not dishonor others frees you to let people be who they are. It takes away any perceived responsibility of having to correct, rescue, direct. Love that does not dishonor appreciates our equality while recognizing the beauty in the differences. Love that does not dishonor others allows, maybe even encourages, people to have different opinions without taking it as an attack on yours. Love that does not dishonor others does not judge. Love that does not dishonor others calls people by name, does not put people in boxes, and does not condemn them for their beliefs and opinions. Love that does not dishonor others loves everybody, without regard to a political party, religion, race, culture, skin color, gender, sexual orientation—just loving the individual. "God is love. Whoever lives in love lives in God, and God in them" (1 John 4:16).

Love that is not self-seeking seeks to do for others. Find good and beautiful things for those you love, as in everybody. Be aware of ways you can seek joy, comfort, and care for others. If you are not self-seeking, not always looking out for number one, you love in selfless ways. "Let no one seek his own good, but the good of his neighbor" (1 Cor. 10:24 ESV).

Love that does not easily anger does not sweat the small stuff or go ballistic. That is no fun for anyone, the temper loser or the wrath receiver. Love that does not easily anger realizes that anger solves nothing and does more harm than good. When anger comes between you and someone you love, deep wounds can leave ugly scars that may never heal. Love that does not easily anger uses anger in the right way for the right things. Like tipping over tables in a temple, anger is directed at injustices. "Slowness to anger makes for deep understanding; a quick-tempered person stockpiles stupidity" (Prov. 14:29 MSG).

Love that keeps no record of wrongs moves on, changes the story, or, at the very least, the tone of the story. It forgives while not forgetting, no bitterness or resentment coming out to play. It just changes the narrative from, "You made me sleep outside" to, "Sleeping outside taught me a lot." Love that does not keep record of wrongs does not bring up past arguments that have already been put to bed; it leaves them there. It leaves the past in the past. It holds no grudges. "Hatred stirs up strife, but love covers all offenses" (Prov. 10:12 ESV).

Love that does not delight in evil but rejoices in the truth challenges the status quo. Stands up for what is right. Seeks justice. Love that does not delight in evil but rejoices in the truth is bold, tough, strong, uniting, not dividing. Love that does not delight in evil but rejoices in the truth says, "I am standing up because I love." It does not go with the crowd; it does not turn away. It speaks up without caring what anyone thinks. "Enough! You've corrupted justice long enough, you've let the wicked get away with murder. You're here to defend the defenseless, to make sure that underdogs get a fair break; your job is to stand up for the powerless, and prosecute all those who exploit them" (Ps. 82:2–4 MSG).

Love that always protects shields from harm. It loves enough to know how to protect and then has the courage to do it. Love that always protects doesn't wish harm on anyone. Love stands in harm's way, no matter the cost. It takes others' illnesses, disappointments, and discouragement, picks up the pieces, and finds a way through. "We who are strong ought to bear with the failings of the weak and not to please ourselves. Each of us should please our neighbors for their good, to build them up" (Rom. 15:1–2).

Love that always trusts takes people at their word, not always looking for ulterior motives or trying to read between the lines. When people love others with love that always trusts, dialogues change. When people know that they are trusted, they strive to be worthy of that trust. Love that always trusts, trusts that you are not alone and don't have to do it all; others are there to share the load. Love that always trusts accepts a helping hand, a word of encouragement, a word of advice, because you trust that others have your best interest at heart. "As iron sharpens iron, so one person sharpens another" (Prov. 27:17).

Love that always hopes never gives up, never gives in. Love that always hopes looks to the future, hoping for a better future for yourself and for those you love, everybody. It loves passionately, prays fervently, hopes endlessly. "Weeping may stay for the night, but rejoicing comes in the morning" (Ps. 30:5).

Love that always perseveres loves through the tough times. It keeps your head up and your eye on the prize. Love that always perseveres keeps going, doesn't turn away during crisis, illness, hardship. It bolsters, upholds, sustains others. Trudging ahead, no matter the conditions, no matter the difficulty, love goes through it, always. "We continue to shout our praise even when we're hemmed in with troubles, because we know how troubles can develop passionate patience in us, and how that patience in turn forges the tempered steel of virtue, keeping us alert for whatever God will do next" (Rom. 5:3–4 MSG).

If this love—the love that Jesus is, that God has for us, wants us to have for others, and wants us to have for ourselves—is lived, there is no limit, no ceiling, no boundaries on what this love can do. No sacrifice too big; Jesus, love in person, made the greatest sacrifice of all, his life. No act too small; Jesus dined with sinners and lives were transformed over dinner. This love, patient, kind, non-judgmental love is strong and powerful, yet gentle and meek. It can tear down walls that have stood for centuries, rip away blinders and expose light, all while veiled in humility and blanketed in honor. Love runs into obstacles but tenaciously pushes through. It is not always easy, but it is always right. This kind of love, this What Would Love Do love, never fails.

 Kɪᴍ Sᴏʀʀᴇʟʟᴇ ɪs ᴛʜᴇ ᴇxᴇᴄᴜ-ᴛɪᴠᴇ director of Rays of Hope International. Her work takes her from her home in Grand Rapids, Michigan, to isolated villages in Africa, small mountain communi-ties in Haiti, and squatter neighbor-hoods in the Dominican Republic. Kim writes stories from her heart, sharing her experiences in life, in love, and her passion for serving. Kim's book *Cry Until You Laugh* details her experience losing her husband to cancer shortly after receiving her own cancer diagnosis, and offers hope to find joy and humor in the hard times.

Between all of her kids and their spouses, there are entrepreneurs, a humanitarian-organization director, a NASA engineer, a NASA administrator, an MD/Ph.D., and a Funeral Director. Kim believes that her eleven grandkids will someday solve issues like social injustice, food insecurity, and sock-eating dryers.

Learn more at kimsorrelle.com.

RAYS OF HOPE INTERNATIONAL

Rays of Hope International, a volunteer-based organization, was formed to empower and support programs that are actively working in impoverished communities as a non-government organization with a mission of inclusiveness of humanitarian aid to all people in need. The primary focus of Rays of Hope is to support projects that encourage self-sustainability, thus helping to break the cycle of poverty within the communities served.

No matter where a person lives—Los Angeles, Grand Rapids, Portland, Port au Prince, Santo Domingo, Ouagadougou, anywhere—everyone has the same needs. Shelter. Food. Clothing. Water. Health care. Education. Rays of Hope is a ministry driven by the belief that working together is the key to meeting those needs. Not changing a culture. Not insisting that this way is the best way. But recognizing needs and helping to make them realities.

The desire of this ministry is to be a blessing to both the people that are helped and the organizations that support them in a socially just manner. Get connected and follow them at facebook.com/RaysofHopeInternational/.

Equips parents to inspire kids to take on social injustice—at any age

"Lisa Van Engen presents an educational manual that not only identifies justice issues, but also offers hope and resources to engage these issues in our everyday lives. Very rarely do we find a combination of passion for the gospel so deep, commitment to justice so contagious, and language and style so accessible in one volume. A valuable resource for adults and children alike!"

—JAMES TANETI, director of the Syngman Rhee Global Mission Center